SEXUAL HEALERS

SEXUAL HEALERS

HIDDEN SECRETS AND TRUE VALUES OF THE LEGAL SEX TRADE

By Madam Bella Cummins,
Owner of Bella's Hacienda Ranch

© 2025 by Bella Shauna Cummins.

All rights reserved. No part of this book may be reproduced or utilized in any form or by any means, except in the case of brief quotations embodied in critical articles or reviews, without permission in writing from the author.

For questions about the book or author interviews, contact Bella Cummins at Sexualhealers2025@gmail.com

Library of Congress Control Number: 2025915610

ISBN for print version: 978-1-7357264-2-7

ISBN for e-book version: 978-1-7357264-3-4

Photos are used with permission of the photographers credited with the photos.

Front cover photo of courtesans at Bella's Hacienda Ranch, by Brandi Betancourt

Note on text: Courtesans and other sex workers interviewed for this book have used work names or other aliases to protect their privacy.

For Lance, my knight in shining armor.

"As someone who was born and raised in Nevada, I have grown up within the statewide environment of legalized gaming and brothels as part of our state's unique history.

"During my formative years, I often heard my very conservative, dear mother speak about why she felt legal brothels were a benefit to our community. She often said that a well-regulated and properly run brothel kept the criminal element of prostitution off the streets and out of our cities. Statistics have shown that to be the case in nearly every county or city where legal brothels exist.

"The reality is that brothels like Bella's in Wells, Nevada, have given more to the local community than just a simple economic boost; they have provided safety and security for the worker and the patron. Our state is, indeed, very unique."

— **Jim Gibbons, Nevada governor 2007-11**

* * *

"It's the 2020s. Bella is all about the female empowerment at her brothel, as women assert their sexual power for the best experience for courtesans and clients, alike."

— **Alice Little, highest-earning legal courtesan in America**

CONTENTS

Introduction:
Let the Sexual Evolution Begin 1

Chapter One:
Warm, Slow Night at the Ranch 7

Chapter Two:
How a Mainstream Outsider Fell into the Brothel Business 17

Chapter Three:
A Modern American Madam Surveys the Oldest Profession 33

Chapter Four:
Bella's Sexual Evolution 63

Chapter Five:
Courtesans' Stories — in Their Own Words 95

Chapter Six:
Madam Bella Raises the Bar 151

Chapter Seven:
Frank Talk with Sex Workers on the Prospect of Legalization 171

Conclusion:
The Time for Sexual Evolution Is Now 221

About the Author 227

INTRODUCTION

Let the Sexual Evolution Begin

As I write these words in 2025, I am the longest-serving legal madam in the United States — 38 years owning and operating a business that is taxed and regulated, and in which independent contractors provide sex and sensual services to clients. I am an expert in the legal brothel industry, which exists in only one state: Nevada. I know how the industry works, and why it works. More than that, I know why it is essential to the emotional and physical wellbeing of the hundreds of thousands of clients it serves each year.

And I believe with all my heart and soul that the legal sex industry, following the Nevada model, should be expanded throughout our nation, because the positive benefits this could provide to our increasingly distressed society are profound.

That is why I am writing this book. And that is the overarching message I aim to impart.

I intended to write this book for many years, and began working on the manuscript several years ago. Now that it is complete, I can say that never has the moment been more critical for it to be published and discussed, and its arguments shared in the arenas of political and social discourse.

Here in 2025, the United States — and our world — are suffering from more existential crises than ever before in modern history. Climate change, economic upheaval, mass migrations and ongoing wars are merely some of the stressors that have fostered economic uncertainty, political polarization, widespread anxiety, narcotic epidemics, and even periodic mass shootings.

What does all this have to do with my book — which makes the case for lawmakers to decriminalize, regulate and, yes, legalize the oldest profession, Nevada style? Well, it has *everything* to do with my book and why it must be taken seriously right now.

While there is no magic formula to cure humankind of the emotional strain of life in the third decade of the 21st century, the "sexual evolution" I am calling for can absolutely help millions of people, immediately.

Of course, I am fully aware of how controversial that statement is. I realize how most people's prejudice, insecurities and fears are instantly triggered by the subject of transactional sex. "Prostitution," after all, is an ugly word. But I am confident that readers who delve into the chapters of my book will come away with a new perspective about sex for money — and the benefits that legalizing the oldest profession, Nevada style, can provide to a hurting world.

FIRST, LET ME EXPLAIN what I mean by "the oldest profession, Nevada style." I am referring to the Silver State's policy — unique among the 50 states of the Union and its territories — that allows legal prostitution, albeit on a limited scale. Nevada does so through taxed and heavily regulated brothels that are allowed by state law in rural counties whose local governments permit them. The sex workers in these brothels must pass criminal background checks and undertake regular medical testing to ensure they are free of sexually transmitted diseases. The brothels' owners, similarly, must be upstanding businesspeople who operate within the letter of the law. As for the customers, their privacy is fully protected.

One benefit to the cities and counties that permit the operation of legal brothels is *economic*. The houses generate room taxes, sales taxes and licensing fees. There also is the ripple effect on the local economy from customer flow at the brothels. Another benefit to a local jurisdiction is *legal*: brothels reduce crime caused by an illegal sex trade.

I coined the phrase 'sexual evolution' to describe a movement I am calling for: legitimization of Nevada-style brothels throughout our nation and world. This mind shift requires the recognition of the vital importance of sensual intimacy to the wellbeing of a society and the individuals within it.

But these aren't the only benefits — neither are they the most significant, in my mind. An unquantifiable benefit is *therapeutic* — particularly for the customers who partake of the brothels' services in this era of widespread anxiety and depression, when mental-health issues seem to be the new norm. This benefit of legal brothels should never be devalued. Neither should the aspect of empowerment that the sex workers at a reputable brothel can realize through gaining economic independence in a world in which women continue to earn less income than male counterparts.

For all these reasons, I have written this book with a sense of duty.

MY QUALIFICATIONS TO AUTHOR this book are as follows. As "Madam Bella," I am in my fourth decade as perhaps the world's longest-serving madam, and one of the few female owner-operators of a business that provides what I term "sensual services."

Any business is difficult to run. A brothel is one of the trickiest. To survive for more than three decades operating a brothel is a feat of considerable dedication. And I have learned so much along the way — not only about best business practices, but about human nature. I have interacted with customers and sex workers from almost every walk of life. I understand better than just about anyone the loneliness of the human heart that craves physical comfort and intimacy, even of the transient kind. And I know just how valuable are the talents and deeds of a skilled courtesan. (*Courtesan* — likely a new word for you — connotes a professional sex worker who is committed to providing the highest level of sensual services.)

In addition to *sensual services* and *courtesan*, I am introducing you to another term: *sexual evolution*. I coined this phrase to describe a movement I am calling for: legitimization of Nevada-style brothels throughout our nation and world. This mind shift requires the recognition of the vital importance of sensual intimacy to the wellbeing of a society and the individuals within it. At its heart, it means the humanization of transactional sex as an occupation deserving the respect and sanction afforded every other legal profession.

THERE ARE SEVEN CHAPTERS in this book. Chapters One ("Warm, Slow Night at the Ranch"), Five ("Courtesans' Stories — in Their Own Words") and Six ("Madam Bella Raises the Bar") provide intimate details of the inner workings of a legal brothel, the lives of courtesans, the motivations of clients, and the challenges of operating such an enterprise.

Chapter Two ("How a Mainstream Outsider Fell into the Brothel Business") describes how I accidentally became a madam, after marrying an older masonry business owner who had a brothel on the side. Chapter Three ("A Modern American Madam Surveys the Oldest Profession") gives a historical overview of transactional sex. Chapter Four ("Bella's Sexual Evolution") lays out my argument for legitimizing Nevada-style brothels in the rest of the country.

Chapter Seven ("Frank Talk with Sex Workers on the Prospect of Legalization") examines the possibility for the widespread legitimization of Nevada-style brothels. It recaps recent legislative

I'm the hospitable madam who can pour you a drink or recommend the perfect party.
Photo by Jason Kelley

bills in New York state and Vermont, Massachusetts, Maine and Washington, D.C. And it shares opinions and stories about the merits of decriminalization and legalization, from non-legal and legal sex workers interviewed for this book.

History illustrates how the world's oldest profession — when properly regulated and operated — has proved to be a safety valve to release many of the pressures roiling beneath society's surface. Sex, itself, is an emotionally charged issue, and transactional sex is a topic that most politicians still treat as taboo. This is unfortunate, because the benefits of brothel-style transactional sex are profound.

The good news is that outside of America, progressive governments have decriminalized or legalized brothels with great success. At this critical juncture of our own nation's history — with most citizens under financial and emotional strain, and with violent crime and mental illness on the rise — it's imperative that the United States becomes realistic and pragmatic on this issue.

If my book does nothing else, it should open the eyes of readers — including elected leaders, and sensible voters — to the benefits of a profoundly misunderstood profession. My mission involves bringing sensual services out of the Dark Ages and into the light, where it can be decriminalized, legalized and regulated like any other reputable profession.

The time is right, and the time is now. Together — with capable courtesans providing sensual services to patrons who benefit greatly from them, and safely and easily access them — the sexual evolution can transpire: making our world a better place.

Let the sexual evolution begin!

CHAPTER ONE

Warm, Slow Night at the Ranch

It was a Wednesday night in June, summery with the Solstice two days away, and I was looking forward to the weekend, when business would spike with truckers and travelers.

That's usually how it flows at Bella's. Weekdays slower? Weekends busier. Or vice-versa. All due to the ever-shifting tides of commerce on the cross-country trucker routes, the weather, the season, the regional and national economies, the calendar of holidays and special events. The calculus — mysterious and complex — that delivers visitors to my legal brothel in Wells, Nevada, set at the high-desert crossroads of Interstate 80 and U.S. 93.

This day, only a couple 18-wheelers had rolled into the lot in the afternoon. After I'd taken over the night bartending shift from Lynette, there'd been a man who'd pulled up in a compact car around 6 p.m. and walked in looking strung out. Short, shaggy-haired and jumpy. Dark eyes darting. He appeared to be in his late thirties. When he mentioned he'd logged a lot of hours "getting across the country," I decided he wasn't crazy or manic on pills. His erratic movements, I figured, resulted from quaffing energy drinks to stay awake at the wheel.

He'd chosen Tandy from the lineup of six ladies in residence this week. No surprise. Little blond Tandy is youthfully pretty and striking, with her high forehead and big brown eyes, sloping nose with upturned tip, pert round mouth and 34-22-30 figure. She stands only 5-foot-4 in her white heels — yet she'd stand out in any lineup in any house in Nevada. Tandy is extremely popular, specializing in "GFE": the girlfriend experience. *Tender, sensuous, nurturing.* A lonely man's warm wet dream.

The haggard visitor's credit card had allowed him to withdraw enough for a half-hour with Tandy, though a second swipe yielded no additional funds. The party had turned out fine. He hadn't caused any trouble.

Now it was just past 10 and another party for Tandy loomed. The guest seemed tentative. He wasn't a trucker hauling cargo on the interstate, or a businessman or outdoorsman passing through, or a tourist primed to sample the sex menu. He certainly wasn't a local, with his long blond hair and black-frame glasses, colorful tie-dye shirt, brown cargo shorts and Birkenstocks. Skinny and thirtysomething, he looked like a cleaner, better-groomed version of a post-hippie camper headed in late summer to or from Burning Man: the massive counter-culture festival that runs for a week through Labor Day in Nevada's Black Rock Desert, 400 driving miles west of Wells. As he sat at the bar sipping a second cold glass of Michelob Ultra, and probably wishing he had an India pale ale to slake his hipster taste buds, he explained he was a "techie" from San Francisco road-tripping on vacation, emptying his cluttered urban mind in the vastness of the Nevada outback, soaking in its far-flung hot springs.

"Nevada has more hot springs than any other state," he was saying. "It's rad. You just need to know where to find them. A friend texted me a map to one called Twelve Mile. It's right on the Humboldt, so you can get all toasty in the hot spring then jump in the river. It's up some gnarly dirt road about ten miles outside your town, so I'm only going out there in daylight. I'm killing time 'til morning."

"Well, you've found an excellent place to kill time here, honey," I said. "Where are you staying?"

CHAPTER ONE

Tandy has mastered her girl-next-door persona and Girlfriend Experience skills, while keeping financial goals firmly in focus. *Photo by Victory Tischler-Blue*

"My Honda."

"How did you hear about us?"

"Google."

"Have you been to a brothel before?"

"First time. I'm an explorer!"

He smiled, as if to reassure himself he had a handle on this situation.

"Well, when you book a party here at Bella's, a shower is included."

"Awesome! I've been thinking about that."

"A *shower*? Is that all you've been thinking about?"

He giggled self-consciously. I noticed he wore no wedding ring — not that it mattered.

Mr. Tie Dye obviously was thinking about Tandy. She'd made an impression. After he'd pressed the doorbell button and I'd ushered him inside with a, "Welcome to Bella's!" I'd asked if he wanted a lineup.

"Sure!" he'd replied, and I'd proceeded to hit the button beneath the bar counter that activated an abrasive buzzer in both wings of the house. The girls in residence this week — Kayla and Holly, Lisa and Rosie, Lacey and Tandy — had traipsed out of their bedrooms or the kitchen, gathered in the parlor behind the plush green curtain cloaking the right entrance to the bar room, slipped on their spiked heels, straightened their hair in the mirror, adjusted their outfits (maybe a negligee, maybe a short dress), then sauntered single-file through the curtain into the bar and lined up facing the young man.

Road-weary truckers are great customers. Here's a semi-truck in Bella's lot. *Photo by Victory Tischler-Blue*

One by one, they'd smiled, locked eyes and announced their names. "Hi, I'm Kayla . . ."

"Would you like a tour from any of these wonderful ladies?" I'd asked. With scant hesitation he'd lifted his chin and pointed a forefinger toward Tandy, who looked as fresh and inviting as the printed yellow daisies on her strawberry-red, white polka-dotted summer dress that was fetchingly tied in a bow in front. As the lineup disintegrated — Kayla and Holly,

CHAPTER ONE

Lisa, Rosie and Lacey exiting back through the curtain — Tandy had stepped toward the man, wearing a coquettish pout. She'd run a finger down the young man's chest and asked his name.

"Would you like a tour of the house, Zack?" she'd continued, hooking a hand around his bicep.

"Uh," he'd said, bravado suddenly wilting, "I'm kind of feeling a drink first."

"You can buy me one at the bar."

As they perched on adjacent stools, Tandy had pressed a knee lightly against his thigh. He'd bought her a glass of white wine.

After their chit-chat hit a lull, Tandy had asked, "So, are you ready for a tour now?" To which Zack had responded, "I kind of just want to chill a bit more, if that's OK."

"OK, enjoy yourself," she'd said politely . . . and gracefully eased off her stool and departed through the curtain, out of sight but not of mind.

A FEW MINUTES LATER, the doorbell buzzed. I admitted a truck driver. Tall and slim. Short-sleeved plaid shirt, jeans, boots. Short graying brown hair. Eyes glazed from interminable hours behind the wheel.

He stood before me in a bit of a daze, vision adjusting to the bar's low glow. I recognized this look. I've driven I-80 between Reno and Wells at least 1,000 times, and likely half as many more, in my years of brothel ownership. Sometimes, when I'm cruising through the sagebrush prairies ringed by distant brown mesas or jagged blue peaks, I'll pass a monstrous wreck of a semi-truck crumpled on its side like a dying dinosaur, lying in a ditch or on a dirt median, cab crushed, long trailer twisted behind. Ten tons of wreckage. Perhaps a casualty of a split-second's driver inattention, or startled reaction to a wayward vehicle veering into his path. Or maybe just the inevitable outcome of too many sleepless, grievous days and nights behind the wheel, driving paid-by-the-mile marathons while coping with the weight of mental misery the world can bear down.

For these sleep-deprived pilots ferrying freight along our nation's highways, truck stops are vital oases where they can fuel up, cool their heels at a bar or slot machine, grab a shower and a meal and feel like a human again, instead of a machine. For those who are lonely, bored or horny and sorely craving fleshly comfort, what truckers label "lot lizards" lurk. (Yes, that's a harsh term, indicating the truckers find these women's behavior to be unsavory.) There is no guarantee these sex-for-pay creatures inhabiting the truck-stop shadows are disease free, or possessed of enough sanity to not turn viciously on the trucker while he's in a compromised position, or seize on a lapse in his vigilance to steal his wallet or phone. (I must add that these women, too, are vulnerable to being ripped off or harmed by customers.)

A legal brothel, though, is a safe haven. The truckers need us, and we value them.

"Welcome to Bella's!" I chirped to the trucker. He passed on the lineup "for now," glanced at the tie-dyed, shorts-clad Zack who was staring into his beer, and took a stool at the far end of the bar.

"How's it going tonight?" I asked the plaid-clad trucker in my cheery madam voice.

"Truthfully? Tired."

"What's your name?"

"Dave."

"What can I get you, Dave?"

"Bud."

He laid a $10 bill on the bar.

"You want one five or five ones?" I asked brightly as I made change from the register.

"Oh, for a tip?"

"We're big on tips around here," I said. "My mother always gave tips. One was, 'Never pick your nose on a bumpy road.'"

He laughed. Zack suddenly seemed animated, too — though not from my silly quip. The presence of the other male had roused him from his reverie. I could read his thoughts:

Parties at the ranch are discreet. Only the lady and her date know what transpires behind her closed door. Privacy and anonymity are the rules of the house, as they are at all Nevada legal brothels.

I don't want that guy booking Tandy instead of me.

Sure enough, he spoke up. "Uh, I think I might like that tour now."

"With the lady you bought the glass of wine for?" I asked, straight-faced.

"Yeah."

On the wall behind, I pressed the intercom button to Tandy's room. "Your presence is requested in the bar."

A minute later, she emerged through the curtain from the parlor. Zack was instantly on his feet.

She grasped his hand and led him across the room to the curtained entrance on the opposite end. This led to the original, older hall, including the two men's restrooms with showers, the VIP Room with its enormous bed surrounded by mirrored ceiling and walls, and Room 2: the Conversation Room.

Outside in the distance, a train whistle blew: two long hoarse blasts, a short and another long, carrying from the Union Pacific tracks beyond the southern end of the parking lot.

Lonesome wails lingering in the simmering night.

PARTIES AT THE RANCH are discreet. Only the lady and her date know what transpires behind her closed door. Privacy and anonymity are the rules of the house, as they are at all Nevada legal brothels.

Bella's is a beacon day and night to guests passing through Wells. *Photo by Victory Tischler-Blue*

Before reaching her room, Tandy's tour had taken Zack from the old wing through the corridor that ran horizontally behind the bar's back wall and into the new wing. At the end of this connecting corridor, turning right leads to the parlor and kitchen. Tandy led Zack left, into the newer hall lined with bedrooms. She showed him the BDSM room at one end, with its big bed, bondage restraints, whips, masks and other paraphernalia.

"This is sick," he said — meaning surprising and intriguing in Millennial Speak.

"My room's down at the other end," Tandy said. "Let's go back to the other wing."

They sat on the sofa in Room 2 of the older hall, the door half-open, as she gave a rundown of the "GFE."

"I'm touchy feely," she said, sitting close, her breath a warm tickling breeze against his cheeks.

Her voice was soft, girlish, sincere.

"I love to provide TLC. It's the girlfriend experience. I like to get *really* intimate, just like a girlfriend would."

Zack's passion was already roused. However, there was the matter of money.

He dug into a pocket of his cargo shorts, withdrew a small wad of crisp $100 bills folded in half.

"Here's . . .," he said, giving the amount.

"This is half what I charge for an hour," Tandy said evenly, counting the bills. She smiled at him, lips glistening.

"Oh, well, if it's possible, can you just give me as much time as you can for this?" Zack asked. "Can you help a dude out? I'm sure you're worth, like, ten times this much for an hour."

Tandy's face turned pensive. He *was* cute. *And* respectful. Respect counts for a lot in the house. A working woman can get very worn down, mentally and physically. A customer's rudeness can be a deal breaker every bit as much as a lack of hygiene or an exceptionally repelling physical appearance. At the least, a crude or offensive remark or an arrogant attitude can up the asking price significantly.

Tandy's smile returned.

"This is my half-hour rate, but I'll do forty-five minutes for you."

"Cool!"

"Let me take the money to the bartender. I'll be back in a moment."

When Tandy returned to Room 2, she led Zack by the hand back through the corridor and down the hall to her room. It looked warm and cozy inside. Zack's curious eyes took it in:

A queen-size bed with sage-green chenille pillows and bedspread. A sea-green salt-crystal glow lamp. A wood stand with three shelves crowded with makeup bottles, tubes and brushes, hair products, and a basket of brightly colored condom packets. Here and there on the walls were large plastic butterflies with pink, yellow and green wings: symbols of beauty and transformation. Tandy had affixed them there, along with plastic wreaths of white daffodils and stenciled words of inspiration: "Life is Beautiful."

First things first. "You can undress over there," Tandy said, pointing at a chair.

Zack shyly removed everything but his briefs.

"OK, come stand here," Tandy said. She kneeled and slowly eased his briefs down, and with a practiced touch checked his shaft and testicles for warts or sores, his urethra for a cloudy discharge. Any sign of a sexually transmitted disease or infection would prevent the party.

Zack passed the genital inspection. Tandy spread a white sheet over the bed.

Forty-four minutes later, my voice issued warmly from the intercom speaker in Tandy's room: "Thank you!"

That was the code phrase instructing the courtesan to wrap up the party.

With a cool wet sanitary wipe, Tandy swabbed Zack's private parts. Then they both got dressed.

ZACK SHAMBLED INTO the bar, cheeks flushed, eyelids drooped, head tangled with a matted mop of what his generation calls "JBF hair." His smile was unsuppressed from his lips to his brows. He was a young man at peace with himself.

I smiled approvingly.

"Come back and see us after your trip to the hot springs," I said.

"Oh," he said with a sigh, "I'll definitely come again."

CHAPTER TWO

How a Mainstream Outsider Fell into the Brothel Business

Though I had zero experience in "the oldest profession," I became — through marriage to an older businessman — co-owner of the Hacienda Ranch in Wells, Nevada. It felt like stepping into *The Twilight Zone*.

Actually, even marrying snow-haired David Andrews was surreal. Neither scenario was something I could have wildly imagined in my teens or twenties. I was born in 1949, the product of a nuclear family so common in the postwar 1940s and '50s, the oldest of three daughters and three sons growing up in the black-and-white Eisenhower Era. As the culture changed during the 1960s, I was hardly a soldier in the so-called Sexual Revolution. Shauna Lynch was a wallflower in high school whose best friend was her horse, and was a tomboy in college, studying agriculture.

Well, life happens. After dropping out of college my junior year, I returned to my parent's house in Eden, New York, and became a bank teller in nearby Buffalo. That was in 1969 (and no, I didn't attend Woodstock). Desperate for a new lease on life, I left frigid Buffalo on a Greyhound to live with my old college roommate, Susan, in Houston. There, I met the apartment complex maintenance man — a cocky

Texan who introduced himself as A.W. ("Ay-dub-yah"). He had a nifty combover, disarming drawl and sweet-talking tongue. A.W. — 27 to my 20 years — was a drinker with one divorce and two kids already under his belt buckle. Naively, I became wife No. 2. Thereafter, my thoughts of leaving were thwarted by 1) getting pregnant, and 2) A.W.'s violent threats.

Finally, I did flee — seizing a small window of opportunity after A.W. had left the house to help a buddy fix his boat. I took what I could pack in the El Camino, grabbed our infant daughter, Shaunia (whose name differed from mine by that "i": A.W.'s brilliant idea), buckled her infant carrier into the passenger seat, and drove off to a relative's house in distant Kansas City, constantly monitoring the rearview mirror for A.W.'s white pickup, which I feared being in hot pursuit.

> I raised my daughter without a dime of child support. I waited tables, fixed TVs and changed lightbulbs as a hotel maintenance worker, and finally moved out to Lake Tahoe, where my parents had relocated.

I raised my daughter without a dime of child support. I waited tables, fixed TVs and changed lightbulbs as a hotel maintenance worker, and finally moved out to Lake Tahoe, where my parents had relocated. I was a horse trainer at a local equestrian center when I met Gary, who had a supervisor's job with a construction company in Reno. He was a sweet-tempered divorcé rising in his profession, full of quiet confidence and hugs. Then he was overpromoted, lost his job and fell into a funk that forced me to support him. When I partnered with my parents in a diner east of Carson City, Gary waited tables. That proved too much for him, and he walked out, blaming me for his failures.

Husband No. 3 was a rebound. Clyde was a gentle bear in his early forties, a heavy-machinery operator for a nearby mining company, who chatted me up each weekday morning at the diner counter. After our quickie wedding, I found out that Clyde couldn't perform due to a prostate problem. Then he took a job in a different town, and we seldom saw each other. I let him down easy, explaining that our marriage had been a rash decision by lonely souls. To my shock, my broaching of divorce was met by a bearish rage. He kidnapped me, burned down my friend's house, and ended up moving into new accommodations: a prison cell.

It was at the diner that I met David Andrews. It was fall 1985. I was pushing 36. My daughter was 12. The last thing I was thinking of was dating. I was the cook, server, co-owner of the establishment: the local girl who was stressed out and rarely managed a smile.

Here I am, 9 months old, with Mom and Dad, feeling perfectly loved. *Photo property of Bella Cummins*

Mom was clearing tables after the lunch rush one Wednesday when a short, round man with thinning white hair and a paintbrush mustache waddled in. Despite his rotundness, he carried himself with swagger, as if aware people followed him with their eyes. His outfit wasn't anything too special, yet stood out. Over a white dress shirt, red suspenders held up his blue jeans, which were starched and pressed. A red bandanna was tied around his plump neck. He swayed from one brown work boot to the other as he made his way to a window table.

Mom took his order: a piece of apple pie with a scoop of vanilla ice cream, and a cup of coffee. I set the plate on the ledge of the food-delivery window.

Sometime later, I peeked over the swinging doors. The guy looked ready to leave. I headed to the register. Face to face, he was shorter than

I was a struggling single mom in 1975.
Photo property of Bella Cummins

I'd thought. We were nearly the same height. But he had a commanding presence. His front teeth were capped in gold. They gleamed.

"How was your pie?" I asked.

"Tasted homemade, as advertised," he said gruffly. He pulled out a $10 bill from a worn brown-leather wallet.

I handed him his change. He pocketed the money — then paused.

"Say," he said, in a casual tone, "if you are ever looking for a place to live, I'm looking for a woman to house sit while I travel."

I was dumbstruck. I'd never gotten *that* line before.

He left without another word.

Ed, a local carpenter, was chuckling on his stool. "That was Dave Andrews."

"You know him?"

"Yeah, he has a masonry business. He lives down in Douglas. Have you heard of that house in Jacks Valley they call 'the Fort'?"

"Can't say I have."

"Well, it's kinda famous. He built it. He's an American original. He drinks a bit and has been married more times than I think even he remembers. So, he needs a *house sitter*, huh?"

"Not funny, Ed."

"It *was* kind of funny," Ed said. "He's always got his eye out for the ladies. How about getting me another beer?"

CHAPTER TWO

"No, Ed. Go home. We're closing until dinner."

THE NEXT TIME I encountered David Andrews was eight months later, on a June morning in 1986, as I stood over the greasy, spattering griddle at a hole-in-the-wall in Carson City called Angie's. My parents and I had sold our diner. Being a short-order cook five mornings a week at Angie's was one of my three jobs to keep Shaunia and me in a small apartment. Five afternoons a week I fixed fake nails on lady's fingers at a salon. Two nights a week I vacuumed football field-sized areas of carpet at a department store, periodically upending clothing racks from the cord catching on them, and pricking my fingers from picking up straight pins by the dozens.

Angie's door jingled. I groaned when I saw Dave Andrews shuffle in. Same white shirt, red suspenders, blue jeans, pull-on work boots (to spare him from bending over), and that red bandanna around the neck. A blue-collar Santa Claus without the long beard.

Here I am, jumping my filly, Sunrise Sierra, in competition in the 1980s. *Photo property of Bella Cummins*

"Hello, Dave," I said, curtly.

"Oh, you know my name?"

He flashed his gold-toothed grin and settled his girth onto the stool opposite me.

"Well, I know your name, too," he said. "And incidentally, I'm still looking for someone to move into my house, watch it when I'm traveling, look after my horses."

The yellow caps glimmered around his front teeth.

As before he ordered a slice of pie and cup of coffee. I served him quickly and returned to the griddle, pretending to be too busy to chat.

At the register, he withdrew a business card from his wallet and slid it across the counter.

"Just in case you change your mind," he said.

Another flash of his gold-toothed grin. He tottered out, the door jingling behind him.

Instead of crumpling the card and tossing it in the trash, I slipped it into my apron pocket.

FATIGUE AND FINANCIAL STRESS won out. That summer, I moved Shaunia and myself into Dave Andrews' "Fort." The house did resemble a fortress, with high, thick, slump-block walls that reminded me of adobe brick, like on a Spanish hacienda. Small logs protruded through the walls near the top, as if built in a previous century.

No longer working three jobs, I swung into the comfortable routine of doing nails at the salon and feeding the horses and chickens at the Fort. To my relief, David — as I called him now — was busy in Carson City or somewhere most of the day and evening. We barely engaged in more than small talk when we did see each other. Even after he canceled an out-of-town trip, he made it clear my "house sitter" situation was secure.

CHAPTER TWO 23

The Hacienda's bar in the early 1990s. Note the Spuds MacKenzie mascot, on the back counter, used to market Bud Light. *Photo property of Bella Cummins*

Eventually, inevitably, David Andrews' made his true intentions known with a proposal. For a variety of reasons, I accepted.

ON THE MORNING OF Saturday, May 30, 1987, I stood on the balcony of David's bedroom looking out over the courtyard and guests below, working up my nerve to go through with the vows. Heavy footsteps on the stairs. David lumbered into the room.

"Shauna, can we talk?"

We perched on the edge of the brass bed. "Shauna, before you marry me, I wanted you to know I'm six hundred thousand dollars in debt. It's really no big deal. It's only zeros."

I was gut-punched speechless.

"We can work together to pay off the debt," he said, patting my knee.

"David," I stammered, "Did you say six hundred *thousand*?"

"Yes, but I've been in business a long time. The only difference between six and six hundred is two zeros. That's it! There's nothing to worry about."

The Hacienda in the late 1980s. *Photo property of Bella Cummins*

He braced his hands on the bed, grunted and hoisted himself to his feet.

"I'm going back down. Meet you outside."

I wasn't brave enough to call off the wedding. He knew it.

An hour later, I was Mrs. David Andrews.

IN THE END, David's accountant, a CPA in Carson City, tossed me a lifeline. The good news, he said, was the masonry business was holding its own. The brothel in Wells, however, was "earning significantly less." The CPA proposed that *I* start overseeing the Hacienda's finances. That frightened me. Never mind that I had never seen this mysterious place and could only imagine what took place inside it. I knew next to nothing about bookkeeping. Still, I accepted the challenge.

I fantasized that this brothel could help us erase the zeros in that $600,000 figure.

The CPA's assistant trained me. We dug through a mountain of paperwork from Hacienda Rooming House, Inc. *Bank statements. Bank reconciliation forms. Spreadsheets. Canceled checks. Cash-register receipts. Credit-card receipts.* I fit the expenditures into their proper categories as deductions on the spreadsheets. *Bar. Groceries. Linen and Laundry. Etc.*

There was a separate pile of bank-deposit slips from the Hacienda's accounts in Wells. With them were rubber-banded receipts cash register at the bar, and credit-card receipts. I'd have to tally them up, calculate how much income the brothel had grossed. The manager was a former working girl named Louise, whom David insisted "was trained by the best."

The CPA proposed that I start overseeing the Hacienda's finances. That frightened me. I had never seen this mysterious place and could only imagine what took place inside it.

It took six months of daily taxing brainwork at the big maple table in the Fort before I had everything in proper order and meeting the CPA's standards to avoid an audit. I understood what was happening at the brothel — and what needed to change.

David finally agreed to make an unannounced visit to the Hacienda. We set off early one Saturday morning, navigating up to Interstate 80 then heading east through the great Nevada outback. Eight hours later, we neared Wells. We descended a bluff and saw a jumble of white-roofed structures and knots of trees in the valley below. We exited I-80 into the town, passing billboards. One had big white letters — "PETRO"; another a black-and-white skunk logo of a Stinker service station. This was a truckers corridor.

We wound around to North Lake Avenue, passing trailer parks, motels and a truck-stop with big rigs filling its lot. We crossed railroad tracks. David made a right turn onto a gravel loop road. At the bottom of the loop was a wide gravel lot surrounded by sagebrush.

"There she is," David said.

I stared out the windshield. The Hacienda didn't look like much. It was a single-story cinderblock building painted white, with a flat black tar roof. It was shaped in an L, with a long wing and a short wing.

Dusk was settling under gray clouds as we climbed out of the truck. I stretched my arms over my head. I was so excited, I ignored the biting chill in the air. My curious eyes surveyed the building. There was a big rectangular sign on a pole by the front door, rising a half-dozen feet higher than the roof. "HACIENDA" it read in black block letters running vertically downward on either side of the sign.

The brothels have been right here for more than a hundred years. This is the oldest part of town. Miners and cowboys got off the Central Pacific train, headed over the tracks to the houses.

"This place is so out in the middle of nowhere, David."

"No, it's somewhere," he said. "The brothels have been right here for more than a hundred years. This is the oldest part of town. Miners and cowboys got off the Central Pacific train, headed over the tracks to the houses."

"And now we've got truckers rolling in," I said.

"There's still miners and cowboys, too," he said. "And hunters and fishermen. All kinds of people come through here. It's a travel corridor, a crossroads town."

A lone semi-truck trailer was parked between the tracks and the front of the Hacienda. Talk about a cold and dreary Friday evening! I followed David to the front door. It was painted crimson. There was a tiny window in the door. David pressed the doorbell button.

The door opened. A short, small-framed woman with close-cropped blond hair stood before us. *Louise.*

She looked to be in her early thirties. She was dressed in jeans and a short-sleeved off-white shirt with a blue paisley print, and brown loafers. She was pale and plain, the light-red lipstick faded on her little mouth. She wore no jewelry other than a tiny pair of pierced-ear studs.

Her eyes widened in a speechless stare.

"Surprise," David said. "Bet you weren't expecting us."

"Well, hello!" she said in a soft voice.

"Louise, let me introduce you to my wife, Shauna," David said.

I'm wearing my derby hat, Halloween 1998, at the Hacienda. *Photo property of Bella Cummins*

I held out my hand. She shook it weakly.

"We just stopped in for a moment, so I could show Shauna the house," David said.

We followed Louise down the hall and turned into the bar room. The lighting was dim, coming from little recessed lights above the bar. The air was mildly sour from the residue of fumes accumulated from the thousands of glasses of whiskey and beer that had been drunk or spilled, and the thousands of cigarettes and cigars smoked, since the 1950s.

The flooring looked equally aged: well-worn linoleum, unpolished for years, except in front of the bar room, which was carpeted, the crimson faded.

A dozen bar stools lined the bar. Only one was occupied: by the trucker who'd come in the semi. I made out black suspenders and a gray-and-white-striped railroad cap. He was sitting on a stool toward the middle, a glass of beer in front of him.

On the Nevada Fringes, Looking for Olympic Geld

The Hacienda (Legally) Markets Games Specials; Fun Visit From the Feds

By Jim Carlton
Staff Reporter of The Wall Street Journal

WELLS, Nev.—And now for a look at that *other* sport and its efforts to play a role in the Olympic Games.

Utah may sometimes bridle at its square reputation but adjacent Nevada revels in being Utah's naughty neighbor—all those garish, spangled Las Vegas casinos and, since, 1971, legalized brothels in certain Nevada counties.

This being America and brothels being, after all, businesses, it makes sense that some of Nevada's 32 legal houses, like those sad Salt Lake City-area ski resorts that got left out of official Games events, would still want to get on the Olympics gravy train.

We decided to inquire, after browsing the World Wide Web and noticing that, though the nearest brothels are about 180 miles west of Salt Lake City, they had indeed caught Olympic marketing fever, even trumpeting a "2002 Olympic Valentine's VIP Party."

The great thing about Nevada's brothels being legal is that if you want to find out stuff about them, the easiest thing to do is to go straight to the police. Nobody's trying to cover up anything. So we wandered into the Elko County Sheriff's Department, on whose watch are two of the aforementioned businesses, Bella's Hacienda Ranch and Donna's Ranch. They sit side-by-side on a dirt road dirt just outside this pop. 1,000 Interstate 80 town whose motto could be: "You Don't Have to be Lonesome Here!"

Olympics-related traffic?

Anecdotally, yes. For one thing, the police say, the number of new sex-industry workers (a term preferable to prostitutes) registering to do business in Wells this month is about five to 10 above normal. Lacking any other explanation (save Valentine's Day), law-enforcement officers hew to an Olympic tie-in.

This is bolstered by an incident last week when, according to Sgt. Dale Lotspeich, a sheriff's deputy working the graveyard shift noticed a van wandering lost on the back streets of town. It turned out to be filled with federal agents who said they were headed for security duty at the Games—a tense job, if there ever was one. They were looking for Bella's, Sgt. Lotspeich says; the deputy pointed his fellow peace officers in the right direction.

We headed straightway to Bella's Ranch to check this out.

Bella's, in fact, looks nothing like the hacienda its name implies. Perched at the end of a dirt lot where an 18-wheeler is parked, it's a one-story rambling affair that resembles a truck-stop motel. Its owner is Shauna "Bella" Cummins, who greets a visitor in smiles and a jewelry-studded red blouse and gold pendant that reads "JFDI (Just Focus and Do It)." A Chicago native who grew up in New York state and studied ranching, she bought the place for $600,000 in 1981 and has since spent "several hundred thousand dollars" to build it into the 15-room service-center it has become today. The grand opening of the addition coincided more or less with the Games' opening ceremonies.

"I never had visions of running this type of ranch," she says, with just the right amount of irony.

Ms. Cummins is all business when it comes to talking about the Olympics. One of her first inklings that the Games could provide a spillover came, she says, when she was visited by a pre-Olympic delegation from a certain Eastern European country last summer. Even she recognized a transportation hurdle—180 miles *is* an Olympian distance to travel. Hence, while many Nevada brothel owners don't like to talk about their business and don't advertise at all, she decided a major Olympics marketing push was in order.

"These three weeks are the most incredible opportunity for the world to know what Bella's Hacienda Ranch is," Ms. Cummins says.

Besides the Olympics/Valentine's Day tie-in, in which customers are entered into a raffle to win free quality time with the sex-worker of their choice, she has aggressively tackled the transportation issue by arranging for customers to be picked up by limousines in Salt Lake and driven in style to the hacienda. She has also concocted Olympic-like competitions for clients and their servers—competitions best left undescribed in a family newspaper.

The bottom line thus far? Ms. Cummins estimates she's already gotten about 100 Olympics-related customers, though such a number is impossible to verify. Unlike at the Games, here nobody checks credentials.

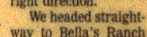

Shauna 'Bella' Cummins

Wall Street Journal article, February 2002.

No working girls were about. I wondered if any had partied with the trucker already — or been unsuccessful and retired to their bedrooms.

We moved to the bar, sat a few stools down from the trucker. Louise was smiling now. Her voice was warm.

"You just drove in, huh? You must have brought winter with you."

"House seems kinda empty," David said. "Who's on shift?"

"We have two girls this week. Peaches and Gina."

I needed to use the ladies room. David led me through a door that led down a long hall that had the same worn red carpet as on the bar, and was even more dimly lit. The left side had three doors with black wooden numbers affixed to them.

"These are the girls' rooms," David said.

The doors of numbers 1, 2 and 3 were open. I peeked into Room 3. It was small and cozy. I was surprised to see not only a full-size bed, a dresser and nightstand, but a vanity and a sink.

The doors to rooms 4 and 6 were shut. David tapped on them in succession.

"It's Dave Andrews," he called out.

After a few moments, the doors opened. Peaches and Gina poked their heads out with drowsy faces. Peaches was a black woman in her late twenties or early thirties, a bit chubby, with short hair she covered with a big wig of straight black hair. Gina looked Latina or Mediterranean. Her red hair was obviously dyed. She had dark features, and a tremendous overbite that made me imagine she gave great blow jobs. She was about the same age as Peaches, had a tiny waist and big bottom.

Both were wearing little tie-front tops, short shorts. They were barefoot, giving their feet a rest from spiky heels.

"How's business been?" David asked.

"Slow," Peaches said in a husky voice.

"Slow, so *far*," Gina said. Her voice was cheery. She could turn on the charm.

"It's the weekend, it'll pick up," David said.

"Oh, we're excited," Gina said.

I kept in mind my reason for this trip: to get a read on the actual business coming in. We returned to the bar.

"So, where's the log kept for the parties, David?" I whispered.

"The ledger?" David said. "There's a sheet over on top of that box there." He gestured with his eyes and chin at a large wooden box attached to the wall behind the bar.

"The bartender writes down each party, with the lady's name and the amount spent," he explained.

The box. Therein lay the answer to my questions.

Louise finally left the bar room for the liquor-supply room to start stocking up for the weekend. I casually walked over to the box. It had slots cut into its top. Two padlocks were fastened to the front. I immediately understood it was a simple system. The cash or credit-card receipts from the parties were inserted into the slots; each slot fed its own little container corresponding to one of the seven bedrooms.

At 49, I was on my own again. However, this time I had a means of financial independence. I planned to take the reins at the Hacienda and run it myself. My career as a legal madam was beginning.

There was a log sheet on top of the box for listing the parties by girl's name, type of party and transaction sum. It was blank so far this Friday.

FAST FORWARD A DECADE. David and I had run through a series of managers before our investment was paying off. With our closer supervision, the brothel was turning a steady profit. David retired his masonry business and we bought a small house in Wells, to be closer to our operation.

Inevitably, David's health declined. His years of obesity and drinking had taken their toll. I became his caretaker as his strength dissipated to a state of feebleness, his coloring changed to light gray and his body withered away.

What kept him going was a big construction project. He planned and supervised our private Hacienda Ranch Road, carved out of the desert, so the big rigs could easily roll into our brothel's parking lot. It was finished after the grader's final pass on a cold day in November 1998.

Later that evening, in our little house in Wells, David vomited up something that looked like wet coffee grounds. It was dried blood, indicated that his body shutting down. We flew back to Reno, drove back to the Fort. A hospice representative arrived. A hospital bed arrived.

A hearse arrived a few days later.

Not long after, I moved semi-permanently to a little house in Wells.

At 49, I was on my own again. However, this time I had a means of financial independence. I planned to take the reins at the Hacienda and run it myself, overseeing all the managerial changes I'd postponed making while David was at the helm.

My career as a legal madam was now beginning.

CHAPTER THREE

A Modern American Madam Surveys the Oldest Profession

When I gained ownership of a legal Nevada brothel in 1987, there were 32 such houses operating in the Silver State.

As of 2025, the number has shrunk to 15 — in part, due to the economic pressures wrought by the pandemic of 2020-23. Otherwise, not much else has changed. Nevada remains the only U.S. state allowing a measure of legal prostitution. And I emphasize "measure."

In Nevada, sex for hire is illegal unless conducted in a licensed brothel, provided by independent contractors cleared through background checks to not have committed felonies, and who maintain work cards through regular examinations ensuring they are free of gonorrhea, chlamydia, syphilis and HIV.

The brothels are not permitted in counties with populations exceeding 700,000 residents. That means that of Nevada's 16 counties plus the capital of Carson City, brothels are never allowed in Clark County: home to Las Vegas. As for brothels in counties other than Clark — it is up to county governments whether to allow them. At present (as in 1987), 10 of Nevada's counties allow brothels somewhere within their borders, and these houses are operating in six counties. Washoe County, home to one of the state's largest cities, Reno, and whose borders stretch to Lake Tahoe, doesn't permit brothels, nor does Douglas County, whose borders also reach Tahoe.

In the counties that permit brothels, the houses are banned from principal streets and within 400 yards of a school or place of worship. They cannot be advertised on a public street or highway, in a public theater, or in any city or town in which they are prohibited by local ordinance.

All this is to say that even in Nevada, brothels are few in number and located discreetly. Legal workers are allowed to engage in sex with clients (with latex condom use mandatory) only within the confines of the brothel for which her work card is authorized.

The constraints on this limited sex-for-hire industry in Nevada generally are tighter than in most other places in the world where prostitution enjoys degrees of legality. In these places, as in Nevada, governments have grappled with how to effectively and humanely handle "the world's oldest profession."

No government, of course, is able to eradicate it, any more than if it could ban the libido. Therefore, progressive officials seek to regulate the trade while protecting workers and clients from violence and theft, and citizens from the spread of disease.

Laws around the world vary wildly — from legal streetwalkers to regulated brothels . . . to death penalties

WHERE ARE THE MOST liberal prostitution laws?

Legal forms of sexual intercourse for pay can be found in on every continent other than Antarctica. Here is a quick summary, as of early 2020, with information gleaned from well-documented articles found on *Wikipedia*, and other reputable sources:

Europe. Laws vary from country to country — from outlawing it in any form, to permitting and regulating prostitution, including in brothels and private residences (although street prostitution typically is restricted to designated zones).

Switzerland fully legalized prostitution in 1942 and has among the most permissive laws. Independent contractors can obtain police permits and pay nightly taxes to work in designated areas — including drive-up "sex boxes" reminiscent of car-wash stalls. The prostitutes have health insurance. Law-enforcement officials and social researchers estimate there are as many as 20,000 prostitutes in Switzerland, grossing $3.8 billion annually.

In 2000, the Netherlands formally legalized prostitution, and regulates it. Germany and Greece quickly adopted similar laws. Germany — where the nation's Federalist Statistics Office estimates prostitution is a $16 billion industry — has state-run brothels; workers receive health insurance and a pension, and pay taxes.

No government is able to eradicate 'the oldest profession,' any more than if it could ban the libido. Progressive officials seek to regulate the trade while protecting workers and clients from violence and theft, and the spread of disease.

A quick rundown of the laws in various European nations:

- In Switzerland, the Netherlands, Germany, Denmark, Belgium, Austria, Hungary, Poland, the Czech Republic, Slovakia, Greece and Turkey, prostitution is legal and regulated.
- In the United Kingdom (excluding Northern Ireland), Spain and Portugal: Prostitution is legal but unregulated. Brothels and pimping are illegal.
- In France, Italy, Ireland, Norway and Sweden: It is legal to sell sex but illegal to buy it and for third-party involvement. This means that clients of sex workers are vulnerable to arrest.
- In Russia and Ukraine, prostitution is illegal.

- **Asia.** In Japan, heterosexual vaginal intercourse is illegal for sale, but oral and anal sex are legal.

  In India, prostitution is legal if conducted in a private residence.

  In Bangladesh, prostitution — including brothels and pimping — is legal, with the exception of male prostitution.

  In Indonesia, there are no clear laws regarding prostitution, so it can be regarded as legal.

  In Hong Kong and Macau — special administrative regions of China — prostitution is legal. In mainland China it is illegal, although erotic massages that involve "happy endings" is legal in the city of Foshan.

  While prostitution has been common in Thailand for a long time — and was taxed during the Ayutthaya Kingdom, which ended in 1767 — since 1960, prostitution has been illegal, despite the industry grossing an estimated $6 billion a year.

  Prostitution is illegal in South Korea and the Philippines.

  Prostitution is illegal in Iran. Punishments range from fines to jail terms, to execution for repeat offenders.

  In Saudi Arabia, all sexual activity outside of a lawful marriage is illegal. Punishments include flogging and imprisonment. If either the customer or sex worker is found guilty of adultery or sodomy, the sentence can be death.

  Prostitution is forbidden under Islamic law in the United Arab Emirates, with big fines and imprisonment for those found guilty, and deportation for foreign sex workers. However, in the UAE's two most populous cities — Dubai and Abu Dhabi — prostitution is widespread. Prostitutes from around the world service foreign businessmen and tourists, mostly in hotel bars and nightclubs. Dubai has been cheekily dubbed, *"Sodom-sur-Mer"* (French for Sodom on the Sea).

- **Africa.** Prostitution is illegal in most African nations, including the most industrialized: South Africa.

In Ethiopia, prostitution is legal, yet procuring (pimping or running a brothel) is illegal.

In Nigeria — the continent's most populous nation — the wording is vague concerning prostitution performed by an individual who does not use a pimp or brothel.

In Senegal and the Ivory Coast, brothels are permitted. In the Central African Republic and in the Democratic Republic of the Congo, prostitution is legal, yet brothels and pimping are illegal.

- **Australia** and **New Zealand.** In Australia, individual states and territories govern prostitution laws. In the Capital Territory, home to the nation's capital, Canberra, brothels are legal. In New South Wales, home to the most populous city, Sydney, brothels are legal, yet pimping is illegal. In the Northern Territory, brothels and street work are legal. In Queensland, brothels and private sex work by a prostitute working alone are legal.

  In New Zealand, street solicitation as well as brothels are legal. The brothels are run under public health and employment laws and workers receive social benefits.

- **South America.** In Brazil, employing sex workers in any way, including in a brothel or via pimping, is illegal, yet otherwise exchanging sex for money is legal. The laws are similar in Argentina and Chile. In Colombia, brothels are legal.

- **North America.** The only U.S. state allowing legal prostitution is Nevada, in licensed brothels. In Canada, selling sex is legal — but not in sexual-service establishments or by soliciting in public areas — and buying sex is illegal. (The client still can be arrested.)

  In Mexico, federal law makes prostitution legal; however, each of the 31 states has its own policies. Thirteen Mexican states allow prostitution, typically in red-light districts.

Sex goddesses, noblewomen ... and outcasts

NO MATTER HOW GOVERNMENTS seek to legalize, decriminalize or criminalize prostitution, none can ever simply get rid of "the world's oldest profession." The history of sex for sale is entwined in civilization. In fact, what researchers term "transactional sex" may be hard wired into the brains of apes — including us "naked apes."

Researchers at the Max Planck Institute for Evolutionary Anthropology in Leipzig, Germany, sought evidence to support a theory that in pre-historic human societies, the most able male hunters had the most sexual partners. In the absence of actual prehistoric humans to study, the scientists observed chimpanzees in a west African national park and found that female chimps offered sex to males in exchange for meat. In their paper published in 2009, one of the researchers wrote the study "strongly suggests that wild chimpanzees exchange meat for sex and do so on a long-term basis."

In ancient civilizations, prostitutes occupied positions of priesthood. Some women partook of prostitution as a trade — and, inevitably, their work was treated as a taxable business. The earliest written records citing prostitution are from 4,500 years ago, in Mesopotamia.

Among us humans, transactional sex has taken many forms in different civilizations for millennia.

In ancient civilizations, prostitutes — female and male — occupied positions of priesthood, engaging in sex as a sacred ritual. In some cultures, women were paid to sacrifice virginity as a rite of passage into adulthood, or as a fertility rite. Then there were women who simply partook of prostitution as a trade — and, inevitably, their work was treated as a taxable business. In some societies, these women were scorned; in others, they enjoyed the status of nobility.

CHAPTER THREE

The earliest written records citing prostitution were from 4,500 years ago, in Sumer, in Mesopotamia (the southern region of present-day Iraq). The cuneiform scripts describe a *kakum* (temple) run by priests dedicated to Inanna, the goddess of love, beauty and fertility. The scripts mention three grades of women in a *kakum*: the first performed rites of sex in the temple; the second were allowed on the grounds and catered to visitors; the third lived on the grounds and were allowed to find customers in the streets.

Fast forward 600 years ...

The *Old Testament*, in the *Book of Genesis*, relates a tale that would have taken place about 3,900 years ago. Judah's daughter-in-law, Tamar, was twice widowed by Judah's older sons and promised by him to marry his remaining son. Judah reneged; Tamar dressed as a prostitute — veiling her face — and sat at a fork in a road where Judah would pass. Not knowing her true identity, he engaged her for sex for the price of a kid goat he promised he'd bring. He left Tamar with collateral: his signet, cord and staff.

Judah's return with the kid to redeem his deposit failed; she'd vanished. Three months later, he heard that his widowed daughter-in-law was pregnant out of wedlock. He ordered she be burned to death. Tamar responded that the man who'd impregnated her was the owner of the signet, cord and staff, which she presented. Judah, abashed, spared her life. She gave birth to twins. His bloodline carried on.

Fast forward 400 years ...

The *Old Testament* tells, in the *Book of Joshua*, the story of Rahab in an event that would have taken place about 3,500 years ago. Rahab was a prostitute in Jericho who hid two Israelite spies who'd entered her inn to collect intelligence on the walled city before a siege. In return for her saving their lives from the town's soldiers, the Israelites spared the lives of Rahab and her family after Jericho's conquest. She married a prominent Israelite.

Moving ahead another 1,000 years ...

Greek historian Herodotus (who lived from 484 to about 425 B.C.), in his *The Histories,* noted that temples and shrines with prostitutes existed throughout the Near East and in Mediterranean cultures. Aphrodite was the Greek goddess of love and passion, pleasure and procreation. Herodotus wrote, with disparagement, that a Babylonian custom required "every woman of the land to sit in the Temple of Aphrodite and have intercourse with some stranger at least once in her life." He noted, "Once a woman has taken her place there, she does not go away to her home before some stranger has cast money into her lap, and had intercourse with her outside the temple." Herodotus added, "… the women that are fair and tall are soon free to depart, but the uncomely have long to wait because they cannot fulfill the law; for some of them remain for three years, or four."

So-called sacred prostitution performed by women employed specifically for sexual rites was practiced in Greek-ruled and, later, Roman-ruled lands. Greek historian Strabo (who lived approximately 63 B.C. to A.D. 24) recorded that in the Temple of Aphrodite in the Greek city of Corinth, more than 1,000 prostitutes (likely slave women freed to be dedicated to the goddess) were in service. These "horae" commanded status. Irish actor and playwright Susie Lamb — who wrote, produced and acted in a 2017 performance piece, *Horae: Fragments of a Sacred History of Prostitution* — said that the horae's practice "wasn't referred to as prostitution then because the concept didn't exist but they were extremely well respected and often became very rich. They were also considered to be healers and seers. Over time this practice, which had occurred in temple or protected areas, became pushed onto the street and gradually turned into something else. The women became poorer and vulnerable."

Sacred prostitution in the region was abolished with the advent of Christianity in the Roman Empire in the Fourth century A.D., when Emperor Constantine shut down temples to Venus, the Roman equivalent of Aphrodite. Prostitutes — female and male — still practiced their trade, just in a commercial, not religious, context. There was, after all, a long tradition for the oldest profession. Solon, the Athenian statesmen who lived approximately 630-560 B.C., reputedly instituted Athens' first brothels (called *dicteria*) and earmarked the earnings to building a temple to Aphrodite. According to a writing of contemporary Greek playwright Philemon, Solon's establishment of brothels was to "democratize" the accessibility of sexual pleasure.

Even though Roman law ended sacred prostitution 1,700 years ago, commercial prostitution thrived in the Roman Empire. Historians note that even Roman men at the upper echelons of society could engage prostitutes without incurring moral disapproval, as long as these noblemen weren't excessive. Scholar Thomas McQuinn, in his book, *The Economy of Prostitution in the Roman World*, wrote that at the time the Roman Empire was becoming Christianized, brothels were considered tourist attractions and possibly were state owned. Prostitutes working for themselves — known as meretrices — registered with the local authorities and wore bright colors and jeweled anklets to distinguish them from respectable women. Some made handsome incomes.

It was a harsh life, however, for the prostitutes at the lower levels of society — those coerced into the work, including foreign slaves and women convicted of crimes sold into slavery. In this ancient form of sex trafficking, there also were "prostitute farmers" who raised abandoned children and forced them into prostitution. It was no picnic, either, for captured women and children in the Muslim world. After the Prophet Muhammed founded Islam in the 600s, he declared prostitution forbidden, yet sexual slavery escaped the definition of prostitution and flourished during the Arab slave trade from the Seventh century into the early decades of the 20th century. Females abducted in Africa or Europe, western and central Asia could end up as sex servants or harem concubines.

In other ancient civilizations around the globe, sexual rituals and/or commercial prostitution existed, including in the Western Hemisphere. In the Incan Empire, the authorities segregated prostitutes from the rest of the population and placed them under supervision of a government agent. In the Aztec Empire, rulers permitted prostitution in the

Cihuacalli (Nahuatl for "House of Women"): an enclosed compound overlooking a central patio containing a statue of Tlazolteotl — the Aztec goddess of purification, steam baths and midwives, and a patroness of adulterers. Aztec priests held that Tlazolteotl could instigate sexual activity while purging the spirit of such acts.

In the Far East, some sex workers were respected courtesans. The *tawaifs* in India catered to the nobility and were performers gifted in dance, music and poetry. Often, they included sex with their entertainment. In Japan, the *tayu* were the uppermost rank of the *oiran* courtesans during the prosperous Edo period (A.D. 603 to 1868) and were trained in dance and music, poetry and calligraphy, in addition to sexual skills. Their art and dress set fashion trends among wealthy Japanese women.

As Europe entered the Middle Ages (A.D. 476-1453) after the fall of the Western Roman Empire, the leaders of the Roman Catholic Church branded prostitution a sin, along with any sexual activity outside of matrimony. Yet in European cities, church officials tolerated prostitution as a way of stemming what they saw as greater sins: rape, sodomy and masturbation. This was a legacy of the pragmatic view of influential Christian theologian Augustine of Hippo (A.D. 354-430), who was quoted: "If you expel prostitution from society, you will unsettle everything on account of lusts."

In many European towns, laws prohibited prostitution within a town's walls yet not outside those walls. Throughout France and Germany, town leaders designated certain streets as zones for prostitution. Brothels run by local governments became common in larger towns and cities across southern Europe after the Bishop of Winchester in central London was granted the right in 1161 to license brothels and prostitutes by King Henry II. The prostitutes became known as "Winchester Geese." One can say they laid golden eggs for the bishop, who oversaw one of the wealthiest sees in England.

On the Italian peninsula, Augustine of Hippo's pragmatism was echoed nine centuries later by priest and theologian Thomas Aquinas

(A.D. 1225-74), who said, "If prostitution were to be suppressed, careless lusts would overthrow society." In his mind, those "careless lusts" included homosexuality. "Take away prostitutes from the world," Aquinas declared, "and you will fill it with sodomy." The revulsion toward male homosexuality held by church and civil leaders in Italy swelled following the devastation of the bubonic plague, which in the mid-1300s killed an estimated one-third of Europe's population, including about half the population of Italy. To counter the widespread same-sex interest by Italian men — what city officials saw as a barrier to repopulating the peninsula — governments encouraged prostitution. In 1358, Venice legalized prostitution and designated a brothel district in the seaside city-state's commercial heart: the Rialto. For the most part, prostitutes in Renaissance Italy were seen as necessary evils. In Venice, they were compelled to wear yellow scarves in public; in Florence, they had to wear bells on their heads, and shoes called *chopines* with heels as high as 23 inches.

Venetian attitudes toward prostitution fostered a rise in station for some sex workers. Women were encouraged to run the brothels, and these matrons gained stature in the business community. There also was a rise in a special class of courtesan who were economically independent and educated: both

Portrait said to be of Veronica Franco, by Venetian painter Tintoretto, circa 1575.

exceptions among Italian women. One of the most famous courtesans was Veronica Franco (1546-1591). The Italian phrase for her station in society was *cortigiana onesta* — which, literally, means "honored courtesan." A courtesan is an attendee of a royal court. Franco, a divorcée, was paid well for her services to an exclusive list of wealthy and powerful men, and her liaisons included one with King Henry III of France, a key military ally for Venice against the Ottoman Empire. The daughter of a courtesan herself, Franco was well-versed in pleasing a man. She also was a leading literary light, penning two volumes of poetry and publishing anthologies of famous contemporary writers. As a philanthropist, Franco founded a charity for courtesans and their children.

An outbreak of syphilis that started in Naples in 1494 and spread through Europe heralded the beginning of the end of the golden age of the Italian courtesan. The prevalence of additional sexually transmitted diseases in the early 1500s furthered the public association of contagious diseases with prostitution. This stance was combined with a less-forgiving attitude of the Catholic Church, and a movement to outlaw prostitution with the Protestant Reformation. The tide had stiffly turned.

Veronica Franco, herself, stood trial before an inquisitor. She successfully defended herself against charges of witchcraft. However, with her reputation irreparably stained, her fortunes floundered and she died destitute.

(Franco's life has inspired me. She was able to forge a life of self-sufficiency and independence in a society in which women were subservient. She divorced the man, a doctor, to whom she was betrothed in an arranged marriage and ended up bearing six children from different men. Her courtesan earnings supported a large household for her three surviving children, their tutors, and servants. A 1992 biography about Franco, *The Honest Courtesan*, by literature professor Margaret Rosenthal became the basis for a 1998 motion picture, *Dangerous Beauty*, which I adore despite its extreme fictionalization of Franco's life.

The pendulum swung sharply in America

THE MASSIVE GROWTH OF cities in Europe and America during the Industrial Revolution of the 1700s and 1800s fostered the spread of prostitution, as vast numbers of people migrated from rural to urban areas and impoverished women sought to survive in the changing economy. Even concerns about the spread of venereal diseases couldn't curtail prostitution. The Kingdom of Prussia, in the early 18th century, instituted a system of compulsory registration and medical examination of prostitutes and licensing of brothels. Other European governments followed suit.

In the United States, despite its Puritan roots, a prevailing attitude toward prostitution held it was a necessary evil. Authors John D'Emilio and Estelle Freedman wrote in their 2012 book *Intimate Matters: A History of Sexuality in America* that prostitution provided an outlet to husbands whose wives neglected their carnal needs — and therefore bolstered marital stability. The authors documented that in the early 1800s, "bawdy houses" in American cities were tolerated by authorities, and laws against individual prostitutes were seldom enforced until the 1830s, when police forces in U.S. cities grew more professional and targeted prostitutes such as streetwalkers.

In spring 1870, D'Emilio and Freedman noted, prostitution was decriminalized and regulated by the city council in St. Louis, the fourth-largest U.S. city. Public-health officials licensed prostitutes who were required to be inspected for sexually transmitted diseases on a weekly basis. St. Louis' so-called "social evil ordinance" didn't explicitly legalize prostitution; it empowered city officials to register, for a fee, prostitutes, madams and "houses of assignation" (such as brothels, and hotels and boarding houses in which prostitutes kept rooms). It also allowed city medical officers (for a fee) to examine the women weekly for disease. (Previously, the governments of France and the United Kingdom had mandated pelvic examinations for suspected prostitutes, as part of campaigns against contagious diseases.)

The St. Louis ordinance also required newcomers to the city, intending to practice prostitution, to register with the police within 24 hours of their arrival. Street walkers and prostitution in unlicensed businesses were still banned, as was advertising for the trade by "word, sign or action" in public places. The St. Louis city council also voted in 1870 to establish a "Social Evil Hospital and House of Industry" in which prostitutes could be treated for common STDs. The hospital was financed by funds collected from madams and prostitutes.

> **In 1870, St. Louis Police Chief James McDonough reportedly estimated there were 5,000 prostitutes in the city — which computed to one prostitute for every 23 or so males of any age. He reportedly quipped that you can make prostitution illegal 'but you can't make unpopular.'**

What spurred such progressive moves? The prevalence of prostitution in the burg on the Mississippi River whose economy was bustling as a steamboat port. A 2009 historical article in *St. Louis Magazine* said that in 1870, St. Louis Police Chief James McDonough estimated there were 5,000 prostitutes in the city —which computed to one prostitute for every 23 or so males of any age. According to the article, the police chief quipped that you can make prostitution illegal "but you can't make it unpopular."

The blowback to the St. Louis ordinance was swift. A groundswell of opposition came from religious leaders, and from women's groups who maintained the ordinance discriminated against women because male sex workers (such as gigolos) weren't required to register with the city. The gender issue also served as a flashpoint for a national women's-rights leader: Anna Dickenson. As the *St. Louis Magazine* article chronicled, Dickenson "arrived in St. Louis to argue that what women really needed was not the right to sell their bodies, but equal opportunities for jobs and education. About 4,000 women signed petitions to nullify the ordinance."

In spring 1874, the Missouri Legislature voted to repeal the social evil ordinance. It was part of a national wave to criminalize prostitution, which authors D'Emilio and Freedman said was led by Protestant middle-class men and women participating in that century's religious revivalism movement, which carried into the 20th century. Led by the Woman's Christian Temperance Union — whose triumphs included the federal prohibition against alcohol in 1919 — prostitution was outlawed in most of the U.S. states between 1910 and 1915.

Yet brothels persisted in many communities in the American West: a legacy of their frontier history.

Mining camps brought 'soiled doves' —
and brothels hatched in the American West

PROSTITUTES WERE THE FIRST white women in the American West, following the trappers and miners. A song jingle from the California Gold Rush era sums it up:

The miners came in Forty-nine, the whores in Fifty-one.
And when they rolled on the barroom floor they produced the native son.

J.R. Schwartz, in his *The Official Guide to the Best Cat Houses in Nevada*, listed some of the colorful madams in San Francisco in the early years of the Gold Rush. They included "Madame Bulldog," "the Waddling Duck," "the Dancing Heifer," "the Galloping Cow," "the Little Lost Chicken," and "Madame Mustache." Their monikers indicate the opposite of physical beauty, but as Schwartz wrote: "Comical and absurd as some of these ladies were, for a while they were the only game in town." Soon, these white women — so-called "soiled doves," "painted ladies" or "lost sisters" — were joined by Chinese courtesans.

After gold seekers had staked vast claims in California, prospectors turned their sights east toward the wasteland of Nevada (then part of Utah Territory), which many had crossed as quickly as possible on their way to California. After silver and gold were discovered in the Virginia Range of northwest Nevada, the new Comstock mining district gave rise to rollicking Virginia City. The painted ladies swiftly followed. The bonanza helped Nevada gain territorial status in 1861. The Territorial Legislature adopted English Common Law, which deemed brothels public nuisances though not illegal. Three years later, when Nevada attained statehood, its constitution did not outlaw prostitution. Political leaders left it up to county officials how to police prostitution.

The sex trade initially thrived in Virginia City. As J.R. Schwartz noted: "The different levels of prostitution went form the lowest slave-trade involving Chinese women in sweatshops and cribs, being paid one dollar per customer, to street walkers and drug addicts selling their bodies, to the house parlor prostitutes (who were making ten to twenty dollars per customer), and the higher echelon courtesans who usually were with only one man a night."

Some madams gained prestige in Virginia City. One was Julia Bulette — famous to this day for her high status; her murder resulted in a major public hanging of the convicted man. But the heyday of Bulette and her class of courtesan ended as Virginia City's wealth brought an influx of non-working women who married the men who prospered from the mines and in the mercantile and trade industries that emerged in town. Yet in Nevada's tiny towns and settlements, the soiled doves were still appreciated and tolerated; this mindset persisted into the 20th century. The sentiment was captured in a quote from James G. Scrugham, who was governor from 1923 to 1927 and cognizant of the state's hardscrabble origin:

"The camps were not for wives. They just couldn't put up with the roughness. ... The miners, some coming in from a day in the drifts, some coming from months of prospecting, hands callused, boots worn, having smelled only sagebrush and sweat ... why, the poor bastards knew the only place they could get a welcome, a smile, a bed with springs, clean sheets, the smell of perfume, was a crib."

It was the same elsewhere in the American West. Prostitution in brothels was not exactly legal, yet wasn't driven completely underground as towns grew and stabilized. Brothels were tolerated as part of the fabric of the community, as long as they were operated out of the public eye. Their owners contributed to the local economy through paying taxes and, often, inflated prices charged by merchants for food and liquor. Meanwhile, residents nurtured the belief that legal prostitution served as an outlet for men and reduced the incidence of rape.

A historical photo of Julia Bulette, the prestigious madam of bonanza-era Virginia City.

The colorful history of brothels in Deadwood, South Dakota — that most iconic of Wild West towns — spans about a century, ending in 1980. It illustrates the pattern of the establishment of brothels in the Old West and their endurance. The 1874 gold strike in the Black Hills that spawned the emergence of a wide-open town in Deadwood Gulch brought a flood of prospectors and opportunists. They were quickly followed by the so-called "prairie nymphs" or "sporting girls." The incoming wagons bearing them had the miners lining up along Deadwood's Main Street to cheer. Some of these women had colorful monikers. "Madame Mustachio" and "Dirty Em" had plied their trade in the mining camps of California and Nevada, and brought their expertise with them.

As elsewhere in the Old West, the women who set up brothels to satisfy the miners, gamblers and merchants enjoyed a strong market.

Deadwood's men-to-women ratio was 200-1 in the town's first years. At the start, the madams conducted business inside tents, lean-to's or covered wagons, but they soon moved their operations into buildings. The working women were usually paid in gold dust (worth about $20 an ounce), and the youngest, most attractive girls were rumored to be able to earn as much as three ounces of the precious matter (equivalent to about $1,400 today) for a single engagement. They'd have to give the madam 40 percent of that — to cover the overhead of room, board and "protection" — yet would still come away with the equivalent of $840. They were providing a valuable service, and were treated as good as gold.

Eventually, the prospectors' pick-and-pan mining played out in Deadwood, and big investment capital flowed in for underground hard-rock mining, an industrial boom that brought more law and order. Yet "the cribs" endured on the west side of Main Street in the above saloons and theaters. The brothels were a mainstay of Deadwood's economy. They also were regarded as a necessary outlet to maintain morale for soldiers stationed at nearby Fort Meade in the 1800s.

Remarkably, the brothels continued operating even as Deadwood's population continually dwindled after the turn of the century as the gold-rush bonanza trickled into borrasca. Deadwood's ruggedly independent residents resisted the reformist tide, and the town's sex houses continued bolstering the local economy during the Prohibition years of the 1920s and the Great Depression of the 1930s. South Dakota state laws forbade prostitution; however, no such ordinance was passed in Deadwood. Patrons climbed the stairs up from the street to reach the second-floor brothels, which were listed as "rooming houses" in the phonebook.

Deadwood's last operating brothel — Pam's Purple Door (previously the Frontier Rooms) — was put out of business after an FBI raid on May 21, 1980. That left the brothels in Nevada as the sole survivors of the Old West legacy. And — since the Territory of Alaska outlawed prostitution in 1953 — they were the only places in the United States where prostitution enjoyed any degree of legality.

How they managed to last to this day is a story in itself.

Quirky events led to legal status for Nevada brothels

AFTER NEVADA'S 19th century silver bonanza tapered to a trickle in Virginia City, and a turn-of-the-century gold boom in Goldfield and Tonopah went bust, the Silver State's economic fortunes and population plummeted. After a drought in the 1920s that devastated agriculture, Nevada's business and political leaders scrambled to rescue the state from prolonged impoverishment. They amended the state constitution to prohibit a state income tax, liberalized marriage and divorce laws, and — in 1931 — legalized casino-style gambling.

What about legal prostitution? The brothels had cropped up in Nevada's mid-19th century mining camps — and were firmly rooted in the towns and cities that sprang from the camps, or that were established by railroad companies. They continued in business as Nevada's maverick mentality made it the most live-and-let-live state. The brothels were not exactly legal or illegal. They were tolerated. While Las Vegas' population lagged Reno's as the principal Nevada city in the first half of the 20th century, its economy was growing thanks to burgeoning casinos, as well as the presence of nearby Hoover Dam. "Block 16," with its cribs for sex workers, sat a few blocks from Vegas' main commercial drag of Fremont Street. Meanwhile, in Reno, "the Stockade" was in two red-brick buildings housing cribs by the Truckee River just east of downtown. The city governments and police in both cities weren't eager to shut down these operations.

The military had other ideas during wartime. In 1942, local authorities in Reno and Vegas closed their towns' brothels under pressure from the executive officers at Stead Army Air Base, near Reno, and the Las Vegas Gunnery Range. The officers didn't want to expose soldiers on furlough to possible contraction of venereal disease. While this curtailed the legal status of such houses in the state's two largest cities, brothels continued operating in rural Nevada locations, benefiting from a gray area in state law: They weren't specifically outlawed.

In 1949, brothels were legalized in Nevada by the state Legislature; however, Gov. Vail Pittman vetoed this, saying Nevada's image would

Joe Conforte, as the prosecution's star witness against Nevada Judge Harry Claiborne.
Photo courtesy of Nevada Historical Society

suffer from "sensational and sordid publicity." That same year, the Nevada Supreme Court gave county commissioners and district attorneys authority to "abate" brothels. But rural officials reasoned the ruling meant they now had the clearly defined option to *not* abate brothels. They could continue tolerating them.

The next significant date in the evolution of Nevada law to permit brothels came in 1970. Two of the three commissioners of Storey County —whose northern border is about 20 miles east of Reno, and southern border expands to encompass Virginia City — voted to pass the first brothel-licensing ordinance in the state (and, likely, the first in the nation).

The driving force behind this — and by extension, the legalizing of brothels in Nevada — was a man named Joe Conforte.

Conforte: the godfather of Nevada's legal brothels

JOSEPH CONFORTE CAN BE considered the godfather of Nevada's brothel industry. In prosperous middle age, he even resembled a Sicilian *padrino*. He was short and pudgy with a pencil mustache, beady black eyes and gravelly voice. He wore expensive suits and elevator shoes, sported a $4,000 hair transplant, puffed Cuban cigars, strolled about flanked by bodyguards, and packed a wallet wadded with $100 bills and passes to his Mustang Ranch — which he doled out to casino dealers, parking attendants and others to whom he wanted to play big shot. He also wielded backroom political clout in Storey County (where the Mustang was situated), and to a degree in the state Legislature. Fellow brothel owners figured that as long as Conforte was around, their industry was protected.

Giuseppe Conforte was born in 1925 in Sicily, and emigrated with his family to America, through Ellis Island, at 11. He lived with his bootlegger father and stepmother in Boston before running away and ending up in New York City. There, the short, feisty youth gained a street gang's respect by beating a foe nearly to death with a television antenna.

Conforte joined the Army and served as a military policeman. Crafty and ruthless, he hustled in the barracks by cheating at blackjack. If a GI got wise, Conforte settled the dispute with fists. Streetwise though he was, the 24-year-old still had much to learn after his discharge in 1950 when he started driving a cab in Oakland, California.

One night, a sailor got into Conforte's cab and said, "I want to see a girl."

"What do you mean?" Conforte replied.

"Oh, I want to see a girl, I want to have some fun, and I want to pay for it."

Confused, Conforte said, "I can't help you. I don't know anything about it."

A night or two later, Conforte had a forehead-slapping revelation after a provocatively dressed woman got in the cab and said, "If you ever have any business, send it to me."

As it happened, the swabbie from before showed up for a ride and Conforte told him, "Hey, now I know where to take you." He drove him to the woman's apartment, dropped him off and waited. After the sailor came out, the woman handed Conforte $3. He'd earned his first commission from the sex trade.

From there, Conforte regularly delivered riders to hotels on the border of Alameda and Contra Costa counties, where hookers plied their trade. His ambition took over and he set up women himself in rooms in an Oakland hotel. After the cops put the heat on, he shifted to a hotel in San Francisco's Chinatown. He was clever, only using Asian women — reasoning they would solely attract Asian customers, and no local cops were Asian. Busted anyway, Conforte looked around for a better business environment.

One night, his fare was an older businessman from Reno, taking the taxi to a boxing match. He was Bill "Curly" Graham: a notorious figure in the Biggest Little City. With his business partner, James McKay, Graham had held major stakes in liquor sales, gambling and prostitution (the Stockade in Reno) when all were illegal in Nevada in the 1920s. They got to talking shop. Graham told Conforte to check out Nevada.

Conforte did. In 1955, he moved to the tiny Nevada town of Wadsworth, 30 miles east of Reno, on the Truckee River along the southeastern edge of Washoe County, and opened shop in a farmhouse. About that time, a named Sally Burgess, 11 years older than Conforte, opened a brothel nearby. Sally couldn't figure out how Joe stayed open while she was threatened with closure. His advice: *When served with court papers, ignore 'em.*

Sally and Joe became partners in the Triangle River Ranch — a group of trailers set near the convergence of Washoe, Storey and Lyon counties. Whenever a sheriff or district attorney in one of those counties declared the brothel a public nuisance, Conforte would have the trailers wheeled 500 yards into an adjacent county.

Conforte's ego soared with his newfound cash flow. He'd dress up gaudily and roar into Reno in a flashy convertible with two of his best-looking girls and cavort downtown. At that time, the Washoe County district attorney was a young lawyer named Bill Raggio — a Reno native of northern Italian heritage with political ambitions. The sight of the smug Conforte rankled him. Raggio repeatedly had the cocky sex trader locked up for vagrancy. A fierce feud developed. Conforte hatched a revenge plot.

Nevada DA's in those days supplemented their income with private practices. Reno had a thriving divorce trade, with out-of-state women establishing six-week residencies in Nevada then securing no-fault divorces. Conforte had the 17-year-old sister of one of his working girls pose as a 22-year-old who'd come to town for the so-called "Reno-vation." The scheme called for her to hire Raggio and have him buy her a drink at the Riverside Hotel downtown, then seduce him. During all this, Conforte would be hiding in the closet. At the right moment, he'd spring out and tell a stunned Raggio that he'd caught him in the act of contributing to the delinquency of a minor. The implication is that Raggio's career would be wrecked — unless he issued a public apology to Conforte for having harassed him.

The plan backfired. Raggio wisely had a friend accompany them to the woman's hotel room, where he secretly tape-recorded Conforte's extortion attempt. Conforte was sentenced to 22 months in the state penitentiary in Carson City. His and Sally's brothel was "abated" — torched under the supervision of the fire chief of Reno's sister city, Sparks. Bill Raggio was in attendance to watch.

While behind bars, Conforte was convicted of tax evasion and spent additional months in a federal prison in Washington state. Undaunted, after his release he rejoined Sally in running a brothel. Now, however, he faced stiff competition. In 1967, a man named Richard Bennet began an operation in the Lockwood area along the Truckee River. The spot was only 12 miles down U.S. 40 (the predecessor to Interstate 80) from Reno and Sparks. Conforte and Sally shifted their business to a site two miles closer to Reno and Sparks than Bennet's double-wide trailers.

In the end. Bennet's trailers went up in flames and Conforte convinced him to sell. Joe and Sally, who had married, opened their new Mustang Ranch brothel, feeling secure it was remotely situated from constant monitoring by Storey County sheriff's deputies based in distant Virginia City. The relative proximity of the Mustang to the Reno-Sparks metropolitan area also meant Conforte could coax cabbies and hotel employees to steer customers his way. Bellmen at the swank Mapes Hotel in Reno were soon telling guests they could find action at the Mustang.

Conforte's next big move was getting the "action" legalized.

How Conforte's crafty maneuvers got brothels legalized

IN 1967, A STOREY County district judge ordered the Mustang to be shut, and instructed Conforte to repay Storey County $5,000 in monthly installments of $1,000 to offset patrol costs to ensure the brothel remained closed. Conforte kept business running as usual — yet paid the $1,000 a month. After the five months were up, he *continued* sending $1,000 a month. The cash-strapped county took the money.

In the 1971 Nevada Legislature, Clark County legislators scrambled to push through a bill to prevent brothels in Las Vegas. It would be tough passing a bill to ban all brothels in Nevada — so they backed a law to prohibit them in counties with populations more than 200,000. The implication was the remaining counties could decide about brothels themselves.

Three years later, the county district attorney told the three county commissioners they needed an ordinance to make the money coming in legal. Conforte recommended the county officials set the brothel-licensing fee at $18,000 a year — too sweet for them to turn down. On Dec. 5, 1970, two lame-duck commissioners — commanding a 2-1 majority on the board — passed what likely was the first brothel-licensing ordinance in the nation. It took effect that Christmas Day.

Conforte's political juice had been felt. Some observers believed his influence extended to Las Vegas. In February 1971, the Clark County DA prepared an ordinance to permit a brothel near the Las Vegas Strip, where the hotel-casinos drew millions of tourists. The Nevada Legislature meets every other year, and had begun its 1971 session that month. The legislators from Clark County scrambled to push through a bill to prevent brothels in their jurisdiction. They feared that having legal prostitution in their county would generate ruinous publicity and threaten the casino industry. Federal law enforcers already were aggressively investigating organized crime in Vegas casinos. The Clark lawmakers realized it would be tough getting a bill passed that would ban all brothels in Nevada — so they backed a law to prohibit brothels in counties with populations more than 200,000. (Clark County was the only county in Nevada that exceeded that mark.)

The law was passed. Yet its implication was that the remaining counties could decide about brothels for themselves. Indeed, the commissions of rural Lyon and Churchill, Mineral and Esmeralda counties subsequently approved the licensing of brothels. Additional counties would follow suit — and the brothels already operating within their borders suddenly had bona fide legitimacy.

A final significant year in the timeline is 1978, when the Nevada Supreme Court said the 1971 state law implied that brothels can be legal in counties under the specified population limit of 200,000. (That limit was subsequently raised to 400,000. Today, it is 700,000. The limit is meant to ensure no brothels are legal in Clark County.)

Conforte's efforts to legalize brothels succeeded, albeit on a limited scale. His legal woes, however, increased.

Joe's final act

IN 1977, JOE AND Sally were sentenced on 10 counts of federal income-tax evasion. She was given a suspended sentence. He faced five years, minimum, in prison. In 1980, his appeals run out and facing 20 years for failing to pay withholding and Social Security taxes, Joe fled to Rio de Janeiro, Brazil, leaving Sally to run the Mustang by herself.

He finagled a return by cutting a deal with federal prosecutors to have pending charges against him dropped or reduced in return for his testimony against a U.S. district judge, Harry Claiborne, who'd been indicted on bribery, fraud and tax-evasion charges. Conforte testified he'd given $85,000 in bribes to Claiborne to pass onto federal appeals-court judges to, in part, overturn Conforte's tax conviction. It later was determined in court that Joe's testimony was fabricated; Claiborne's trial ended in a hung jury.

Joe resumed running the Mustang. However, he still owed a large back-tax bill. In September 1990, IRS agents seized the brothel for about $13 million in back taxes, including interest and penalties. When the federal bankruptcy-court trustee arrived to prepare for running the ranch on behalf of the government, Conforte already had cleaned out the till and taken the workers' health cards. Women were jumping out windows to flee.

The trustee eventually gave up on running the ranch. The IRS auctioned the Mustang and its goods for $1.5 million to Mustang Properties Inc. In Nevada, corporate shareholders' names are allowed to remain secret. Was Conforte, himself, one of the owners? One thing was certain: He was back at the ranch as its general manager. He remained in that post until announcing his retirement in August 1991, declaring he'd served more than 1.5 million customers in his 38-year career.

Sally died in September 1992. By this time, Joe was back living in Brazil, saying he feared returning to the United States because the feds would pursue him again. Indeed, a federal grand jury handed up a number of indictments in 1995 and 1998 against him, including for bankruptcy fraud. Yet a Brazilian court ruled in 1999 that the extradition treaty between the country and the United States did not cover bankruptcy fraud.

The federal government took ownership of the Mustang I and adjacent Mustang II brothels, closed them and auctioned off their assets. The name "Mustang" endured, however, on a brothel. Real-estate developer Lance Gilman secured the rights to the name. Gilman had bought the Mustang buildings on eBay for $145,100 and relocated them to his Wild Horse Adult Resort & Spa brothel five miles east of where the Mustang property had stood. His claim to the Mustang Ranch trademark was upheld in court, and his brothel bears that name today.

As for Joe Conforte? He reportedly passed away in March 2019 in Brazil, at the ripe old age of 93.

Nevada brothels always face vocal adversaries

AS OF 2025, there are 15 legal brothels operating in six of the 10 Nevada counties that permit them. Forty-nine years after state lawmakers allowed brothels to be permitted in rural counties, they're never free of the threat of being banned in those counties, or outlawed at the state level. Anti-brothel groups and lawmakers periodically target the industry.

In 2018, for example, voters in Lyon County — home to four legal brothels, including the best-known one in the nation, the Moonlite BunnyRanch, in Mound House — voted on an advisory question that reached the ballot after a petition drive by activists who said banning the brothels would help curb sex trafficking. Those who opposed the question said the ban would cost Lyon County nearly $400,000 in revenue from licenses and fees from the brothels — funds earmarked to purchasing vehicles for the sheriff's office — and it would put hundreds of people out of work.

My registration card from the city of Wells after I was added to the brothel license. *Photo property of Bella Cummins*

That November, a wide majority of voters said nay to the initiative.

On the state level, a bill to ban the brothels was introduced into

Helen Marvel opens a gift during her 80th birthday celebration, at the Hacienda. *Photo by Bella Cummins*

the Senate Judiciary Committee in the 2019 session of the Nevada Legislature. Senate Bill 413 — sponsored by Republican senators Joseph Hardy and Pat Spearman — aimed to outlaw legal brothels. Its wording prohibited the "granting of a license for a house of prostitution," and removed "an exemption from criminal liability for prostitution committed in a licensed house of prostitution; eliminating exemptions from certain laws for licensed houses of prostitution." If enacted, violators could be jailed, fined or both.

The bill didn't make it out of committee.

Another legal attack on Nevada's brothels in 2019 was a federal lawsuit asserting that the industry flouted two federal laws that ban human trafficking across state lines for commercial sex acts. The suit was filed by a lawyer for three Texas women who claimed they were victims of sexual violence in Nevada and other states. Their lawyer, Jason Guinasso, contended that if Nevada didn't permit legal brothels, his clients would not have been trafficked to the state.

In October 2019, U.S. District Judge Miranda Du, in Reno, dismissed the suit. In her ruling, Judge Du wrote: "That plaintiffs were unlawfully forced into prostitution and sex trafficked in Nevada and other states is not sufficiently traceable to Nevada laws ... as opposed to other factors, namely the illicit behaviors of private bad actors."

The specter of legalization hangs on the horizon

WHILE MOVEMENTS TO OUTLAW Nevada's brothels continue, an opposite movement — to decriminalize or legalize prostitution — also seems to be gaining sway around the United States. Progressive activists and some elected officials see this as a sound and humane way to eradicate the nasty aspects of illegal sex work that harm communities and endanger both sex workers and their clients. These nasty aspects include sex trafficking.

As the 2020 presidential race heated up, several candidates in the large field of Democratic hopefuls expressed support for some type of decriminalization of sex work. Among them were Pete Buttigieg, the 37-year-old former mayor of South Bend, Indiana, who was among the leaders in his party's polls in early 2020, and whose campaign stressed his next-generation appeal. Buttigieg told journalists that — while he wasn't calling for the legalization of sex work — the time was ripe for a serious national conversation on the issue. Buttigieg indicated his willingness to support protections for sex workers and said the subject of sex work "needs to be part of a larger conversation about how we treat sex workers and all of the reasons why this society hesitates to embrace the idea of sex work."

Another 2020 Democratic contender, then California U.S. Sen. Kamala Harris (and later, Vice President, after becoming the running mate of party nominee Joe Biden), had gone on record in a February 2019 interview with *The Root*, a news-and-culture website dedicated to reporting on African-American issues, that she conditionally supports decriminalization of transactional sex, saying: "when you're talking about consenting adults, I think that yes we should really consider that we can't criminalize consensual behavior as long as no one is being harmed."

This national discourse seems long overdue. As throughout American history — and world history — sex for money survives with or without legality.

Illicit prostitution can be engaged in some massage parlors and via escort services, in illegal brothels and with call girls and streetwalkers. Writers for the website and book-publishing company Havocscope.com — who collection information from government reports, news articles and academic papers — report that an estimated $14.6 billion in revenue from prostitution is generated annually in the United States, placing it fifth in the ranking of nations, behind Germany ($18 billion in a legal industry), Japan ($24 billion), Spain ($26.5 billion), and China ($73 billion).

The Paris-based, nonprofit Scelles Foundation, whose proclaimed mission is "to fight against the system of prostitution and the exploitation of prostituted persons," estimated in a 2012 report that there are 1 million prostitutes in the United States (and 40 million to 42 million in the world). A 2004 poll by Kantar TNS, a global-market research company, reported that in the United States, 15 percent of all men have paid for sex and 30 percent of single men over age 30 have paid for sex.

All this is to say that the world's oldest profession continues to flourish in America. History has taught us that simply outlawing it doesn't protect the public; rather, it drives sex-for-sale further into the shadows.

History also has taught us that legalizing and regulating prostitution doesn't eradicate the illegal trade. Yet, it surely is the best option for protecting everyone involved from crime and disease.

I would like to believe that as more people become truly educated on the issue, they will understand that legalization is the best course. My hope is that you — the reader — will be among these supporters of legalization, after reading the following section: *Bella's Sexual Evolution*.

CHAPTER FOUR

Bella's Sexual Evolution

"We call our country home of the brave and land of the free, but it's not. We give a false portrayal of freedom. We're not free — if we were, we'd allow people their freedom. Prohibiting something doesn't make it go away. Prostitution is criminal, and bad things happen because it's run illegally by dirt-bags who are criminals. If it's legal, then the girls could have health checks, unions, benefits, anything any other worker gets, and it would be far better."

— Jesse Ventura, in a *Playboy* magazine interview in 1999, after being elected governor of Minnesota

"Le sens commun n'est pas si commun."
— Voltaire

To translate the famous saying by Voltaire, "Common sense is not so common." Keeping all forms of sex-for-sale illegal is nonsensical. Throughout human history, the world's oldest profession has survived, and thrived — even where it has been outlawed.

In its illegal forms, prostitution has been a source of crime and violence, disease and despair. Where it has been legalized and effectively regulated by governments, multiple benefits have accrued for all parties involved.

When Alexa Albert, a medical student with a book-publisher's contract, began interviewing and shadowing sex workers at the old Mustang Ranch and other Nevada brothels in the 1990s, she was biased against legal prostitution. As she wrote in *Brothel: Mustang Ranch and Its Women*, published by Ballantine Books in 2001: "I fundamentally believed prostitution was a dehumanizing, objectifying business that did women real damage." Her research over seven months changed that view. Here is what she wrote near the end of her book: "Legal brothels are one alternative in dealing with prostitution. However disturbing the idea of commercial sex may be to some of us, it's naïve to believe that prostitution can ever be eliminated. The demand will be met with supply one way or another, no matter what is legislated. Turning our backs on the women (and men) who do this work may be far more immoral — even criminal — than prostitution itself. Only when we recognize and validate the work of professional prostitutes can we expect them to practice their trade safely and responsibly."

My unwavering belief — based on 38 years as a brothel owner — is that the Nevada model of legalized prostitution should be expanded to our entire nation, and our world.

Spreading the legalization of the Nevada model for prostitution — I prefer the term "sensual services," as I will explain later — is a key part of a campaign I call "sexual evolution." I spell out the case for this campaign on the following pages.

Nevada-style brothels can revolutionize the sex-for-sale industry

IN THE NEVADA MODEL for legal prostitution, sex-for-sale is lawfully available only in licensed brothels. These houses are closely monitored by local law-enforcement and health officials and located outside of large population centers and away from heavy vehicular or foot traffic. The services are provided by independent contractors who have undergone thorough criminal-background checks by law enforcement. These independent contractors are tested weekly for gonorrhea and chlamydia, monthly for syphilis and HIV. They perform oral or vaginal sex (and, according to the individual worker's preference, anal sex) only with the use of latex condoms: a policy that brothel owners voluntarily instituted in 1986, and the state government mandated in 1988.

The services are provided by independent contractors who have undergone thorough criminal-background checks. They are tested weekly for gonorrhea and chlamydia, monthly for syphilis and HIV.

These precautions add up to this advantage for Nevada's legal brothels over illegal forms of sex-for-sale:

The risk of spreading sexually transmitted diseases is extremely low in legal brothels.

Since Nevada began requiring screenings of sex workers at brothels for sexually transmitted diseases or infections in 1986, not *one* documented case of transmission of HIV — the virus that causes AIDS — has occurred at a legal brothel in the Silver State. In addition, the rates of gonorrhea, chlamydia and syphilis infection among sex workers tested during their stints in Nevada brothels are below the state's average for all populations; indeed, the rates for these STDs or STIs are close to *zero*. The rates contrast starkly with that of sex workers elsewhere, including porn actors.

In 2010, six public-health experts — whose affiliations included Johns Hopkins, UCLA and the Los Angeles County Department of Public Health — studied a group of 168 adult-film performers in Los Angeles County. The researchers' report, released in 2012, found that 28 percent (47 performers) tested positive for either gonorrhea or chlamydia, or both. The researchers attributed the vast difference in the rate of positive tests between the L.A. porn workers and Nevada brothel workers to the fact that the brothel workers wear latex condoms. Among the porn actors, consistent condom use was "very low" either on or off the sets, the researchers said.

Want a more graphic statistic?

A 1998 study on sex workers in Australia — where some states and territories have legalized brothels — compared the prevalence of sexually transmitted bacterial infections between two study groups: illegal street workers and legal brothel workers. The researchers found the rate to be 80 times higher in the 63 illegal street prostitutes than in the 753 sex workers in legal brothels.

Common sense dictates that legal, regulated prostitution that includes government-mandated health examinations, and the required use of latex condoms, is a better model for protecting sex workers and clients from spreading sexually transmitted diseases or infections than is the model of keeping all prostitution illegal. You can't force health checks and condom use on streetwalkers who work illegally, or on sex workers who work illegally in establishments such as massage parlors. Or on escorts, high-end call girls, outcall entertainers, or workers in nightclubs or bars, casinos or hotels who engage in prostitution with customers on the side, or are unofficially contracted by work-site managers to take care of preferred customers on the sly.

On *any* sex worker, that is, who works without governmental sanction.

However, you *can* force exams and (with careful monitoring) compliance with latex-condom use on sex workers employed in regulated brothels in which every sex worker is required to maintain a license and a work card in order to service clients. In this system, the workers must clear tests for STDs each time before coming to work at a brothel, and must remain STD free in regular tests while working at the brothel.

A skeptic may question whether legal brothels have any significant effect on diminishing illegal prostitution — including the spread of STDs. After all, the various forms of illegal prostitution continue in Nevada, despite the existence of legal brothels. To which I reply:

Were there more legal brothels in Nevada — and were they allowed to operate in more jurisdictions — more people would patronize them instead of seeking illicit sex-for-sale.

Unfortunately, legal brothels are permitted only on a very limited basis in Nevada. As I've noted, they are prohibited in counties with populations exceeding 700,000 residents. That means they are automatically banned in Clark County (home to Las Vegas), whose population accounts for 74 percent of Nevada's population of 3.25 million people (not to mention about 56 million annual tourists). Only county governments in Nevada's smaller counties can approve allowing brothels — and as of this writing in 2025, only 10 such rural counties do (and brothels are only operating six). What's more, the governments of cities within those counties can ban brothels. Within the counties that *do* permit brothels, the houses' locations are severely restricted to keep them out of the public eye. The closest legal brothel to the Las Vegas Strip (heart of the hotel-casino industry in Nevada's largest metropolitan area) is 60 miles away in Nye County. The closest brothel to downtown Reno, in one Nevada's largest metropolitan areas (which is in Washoe County, where brothels are illegal), is 17 miles away in Storey County. Residents or visitors to the Nevada (eastern) side of Lake Tahoe, an international tourist destination whose western side falls within California's borders, cannot find a legal brothel thereabouts because Washoe County and Douglas County — whose borders encompass Tahoe's eastern shore — outlaw all forms of prostitution.

There are approximately 30 brothel licenses available in Nevada. As of this writing, 15 of those licenses are being utilized. For perspective: Nevada is the seventh-largest U.S. state in terms of geographic size: 110,572 square miles. That computes to one legal brothel per 5,529 square miles. There are more strip clubs (25) in the Las Vegas metropolitan area than there are legal brothels in the entire state.

My belief is that if legal brothels *were* permitted in the counties that are home to Las Vegas, Reno and the Nevada side of Lake Tahoe, the number of illegal sex workers in those areas would decline. And that would mean a decline in the incidence of STDs, as well as other ills associated with illegal sex work.

University researchers concluded that legal sex workers report less violence and a heightened sense of security working in the brothel industry than plying their trade illegally in other venues. This is because of both the legality of the occupation and the safety of working in the confined community space of a brothel.

What would *increase* would be the tax dollars and licensing fees going to local governments.

Which brings me to my next point:

Legal brothels benefit local economies.

According to a report, "Sex Industry and Sex Workers in Nevada," published in 2012 by three researchers at the University of Nevada, Las Vegas, legal brothels in Nevada generate approximately $35 million to $50 million in profits a year, and the brothels serve approximately 400,000 clients a year.

The UNLV researchers listed revenues going to county or city governments from brothels paying work-card, application and licensing fees, and room and liquor taxes. The figures from the U.S. Bureau of the Census used in the report were from 2006, the most recent year for which data were available to the researchers. The three-highest totals of local-government revenue from brothels: $353,800 in Lyon County, which had four brothels; $178,750 in Storey County, which had two brothels; $149,313 in Nye County, which had four brothels. For perspective, consider that the population of Storey County in 2006 was 4,110. The county government's take from taxes and fees from the brothels amounted to $43.49 per resident.

This is governmental revenue that wasn't collected from local residents — unlike property, sales or gasoline taxes.

It also must be noted that brothels have an *indirect* positive economic impact on counties. Brothels typically cater to tourists and travelers. Leisure dollars these visitors spend are not only in brothels — they are in other businesses, such as hotels and motels, restaurants and service stations that are in proximity to the brothels or along the routes to or from the brothels. In addition, the brothel owners buy food, liquor and other goods from area vendors, and brothel workers, off shift, patronize area retailers. So, the cumulative economic impact of brothels may be significant in rural counties.

Brothels also are employers. Bartenders, cooks and maintenance workers are typically hired from the local population. As for the working conditions in a legal brothel, here is another factor in favor of them:

Legal brothels are safe environments for sex workers.

In their "Sex Industry and Sex Workers in Nevada" paper, the UNLV researchers concluded: "Legal sex workers report less violence and a heightened sense of security working in the brothel industry than plying their trade illegally in other venues. This is because of both the legality of the occupation and the safety of working in the confined community space of a brothel."

An earlier study by UNLV researchers, "Violence and Legalized Brothel Prostitution in Nevada: Examining Safety, Risk and Prostitution Policy," published in 2005, interviewed 40 prostitutes and collected surveys from an additional 25. Their combined working experience had been in 13 of Nevada's legal brothels between 1998 and 2002. Only one of the 40 interviewees reported having been victimized by violence in one of the brothels; 21 of the 25 who filled out surveys considered their jobs safe.

In contrast, the "risk of violent victimization" was rated very high for street workers — who typically engage with clients in motor vehicles, alleys and other unsecured areas. Outcall-referral workers, and bar or casino workers performing sex on the side with customers, were rated at low to moderate risk.

In Chapter Five, "Courtesans' Stories — in Their Own Words," of this book, Lisa and Rosie — two women who've worked for me at Bella's Hacienda Ranch — relate frightening incidents as escorts. Lisa was working for an escort service in a big city on the East Coast, and by habit avoided responding to calls from bad parts of town. One night, however, she accepted a call to an apartment building in what she called a "borderline" area. When she asked the client for money, he held a knife to her throat and attempted to get his party forcibly for free. Lisa struggled; fortunately, she escaped without physical injury.

A courtesan picked from a lineup chats with a guest before taking him on a house tour.
Photo by Victory Tischler-Blue

Rosie was assaulted, too. After posting an ad on an online escorting site in San Francisco, she did her best to vet clients who texted her on the site's app. Rosie always insisted the client meet up with her first in a public area. During one of these dates, the man talked Rosie into agreeing to accept half-payment up front, with the remainder to be paid at the end of the party. When that point came, he seized her throat. Rosie agreed to waive the rest of the money.

These experiences prompted both ladies to come to work at my brothel in Nevada. Similar experiences have spurred a great many other women to pursue sex work at Nevada's brothels, rather than test their luck outside the law.

Studies from reputable researchers have yielded sobering statistics about the dangers to illegal sex workers:

- Among 130 street prostitutes interviewed in San Francisco, 82 percent had been physically assaulted, and 68 percent raped, since entering that line of work; 55 percent had been assaulted by customers, with 46 percent raped by customers. Sixty-eight percent met the criteria for post-traumatic stress disorder.

- Among 100 prostitutes of Asian ethnicity working in one of the 12 massage parlors in San Francisco, 62 percent had been beaten by a customer, 45 percent had been threatened.

- Among 222 women interviewed, who worked in different venues, outdoor or indoor, in prostitution in the Chicago metropolitan area, regardless of the prostitution activity, "high percentages . . . had experienced violence while engaged in prostitution," with the violence coming most often from customers but also from "pimps, intimate partners, managers, police officers, and neighbors." Among the findings were that almost 25 percent of women in "drug houses" had been raped more than 10 times, and 21.4 percent of women in escort services were raped more than 10 times. There also were large percentages of women who had to hand over a cut of their earnings to someone else (a pimp). About 50 percent of women in escort services, 44 percent of women in drug houses and 41 percent of street workers gave up a cut of their earnings, with most believing they would be harmed if they didn't.

Studies of illegal prostitutes in foreign countries — from the United Kingdom and South Africa, Thailand and Zambia, Israel, Venezuela and elsewhere — also have shown sex workers to have suffered significant rates of violence in their trade. It is a tragic reality for sex workers where the profession is outlawed that violence is a constant risk. So is the possibility of arrest.

It is worth noting that in jurisdictions where legal brothels exist in Nevada, the number of arrests for prostitution is extremely low. It could be because anti-vice law enforcement is not as vigorous in these areas, or because illegal forms of sex-for-sale shy away from vicinities of legal brothels, or because other factors are in play. It would require further study. Nonetheless, in Nevada's most-populous county — Clark — legal brothels are banned. And the arrest statistics for prostitution in Clark County are much higher than the national average.

The UNLV researchers' "Sex Industry and Sex Workers in Nevada" report included arrest statistics for "Prostitution/Commercialized Vice" from the Federal Bureau of Investigation for the year 2009. The total number for the United States was 71,400, which computed to a rate of 23 per 100,000 people. For Clark County — home to the Las Vegas Strip and a booming illicit-sex industry that contributes to the area's nickname "Sin City" — the total was 4,484 (236 per 100,000 people): about 10 times the national average.

This was in stark contrast to Nevada's rural counties. For Nye County (home to five brothels), the total of prostitution-related arrests in 2009 was 1 (2 per 100,000 people). For *all other* Nevada counties except for Washoe County (where brothels are banned), there were zero arrests. In Washoe County — home to the Reno-Sparks metropolitan area (second-largest in the state) — the total of prostitution arrests was 77 (19 per 100,000 people). This was a bit lower than the national average. One possible explanation for Washoe's relatively low rate could be the close proximity of the county's major cities, Reno and Sparks, to legal brothels.

In 2009, two legal brothels sat a mere 17 miles from Reno. These were the Mustang Ranch and the now-defunct Wild Horse Ranch in Storey County. There also were four legal brothels located about 40 miles away from Reno, in Lyon County: the Moonlite BunnyRanch, Sagebrush Ranch, Kit Kat Ranch, and Kitty's (now the Love Ranch).

David H. Rodgers, a criminal-justice graduate student at Florida State University in 2010, produced a master's thesis: "The Viability of Nevada's Legal Brothels as Models for Regulation and Harm Reduction in Prostitution." In his abstract, Rodgers wrote: "Studies indicate these brothels are effective at controlling the violence, sexually transmitted diseases or infections, and community disorder typically associated with prostitution. What remains unknown is whether they deter demand for illegal prostitution, which remains plagued by these harms."

Any public policy strategy aimed at alleviating the worst effects of illegal prostitution in metropolitan areas with legal, regulated prostitution will have to go beyond legalizing brothels exclusively in rural counties. The big cities need brothels.

("Community disorder" includes violence, drug abuse, and disturbance of the peace. Envision police sirens, hypodermic needles littering the sidewalk, aggressive men approaching women on the sidewalk or calling to them from car windows.)

Rodgers opined that legal prostitution "may have potential as a preferable alternative to black market prostitution that suppresses the demand for the black market. However, there is not yet adequate data to conclusively determine if it has the desired effect on the black market. One thing is clear, though. There are many prostitution consumers in Las Vegas who are not content to drive to legal brothels in neighboring counties. Whatever the reasons for this, and convenience is almost certainly one, and whatever their other merits, the legal brothels in Nevada's rural counties hardly present as an adequate solution to the ills of black market prostitution in its urban areas. Clearly, any public policy strategy aimed at alleviating the worst effects of illegal prostitution in metropolitan areas with legal, regulated prostitution will have to go beyond legalizing brothels exclusively in rural counties."

I agree with that conclusion. The big cities need brothels.

Ironically, the fears of state lawmakers from Las Vegas that a move was afoot to license a legal brothel in that city was the impetus for them, at the 1971 session of the Nevada Legislature, to lead the drive to outlaw legal brothels in counties with large populations. In this way, the Las Vegas lawmakers kept the legal brothels out of Clark County, while the Legislature gave the rest of Nevada the option to legalize them. However, illegal prostitution thrives in the Las Vegas metro area — and does not elsewhere in Nevada.

The Clark County lawmakers who kept legal brothels banned were serving the wishes of the owners of Vegas hotel-casinos. The gambling magnates traditionally oppose permitting legal brothels on their tourist turf, saying such businesses would tarnish "Sin City's" image. Yet illegal sex workers are hardly invisible on the Strip or downtown. Dozens of escort services, modeling services and "entertainers" are listed online or in the local phone book. Escorts posing as single women lounge at hotel nightclubs and casino bars, nicely dressed and unaccompanied by a man. Just walking outside of hotels, you are likely to encounter someone handing out fliers promoting "exotic dance."

George Washington University sociology professor Ronald Weitzer argued in a chapter, "Sex Work: Paradigms and Policies," of the book he edited, *Sex for Sale: Prostitution, Pornography, and the Sex Industry*, that for authorities in Las Vegas — and *any* urban area — to effectively enforce "harm reduction" related to unlawful sex work, "the legal avenue for prostitution would have to be in effect in the areas where the ill effects of illegal prostitution are to be suppressed." Weitzer explained that the options for this legal avenue include "vetting and licensing business owners, registering workers, zoning street prostitution, mandatory medical exams, special business taxes, or officials' periodic site visits and inspections of legal establishments."

These are policies that Nevada's rural jurisdictions enforce on legal brothels. As Weitzer concluded: "It is feasible that Nevada's brothel system would be effective if legalized in urban areas."

It's an option whose time has come, because:

Legalizing sex-for-sale is part of a global trend.

A growing movement around the world seeks to address the most harmful aspects of sex-for-sale by legitimizing forms of prostitution and protecting the workers. In 2013, the United Nation's Global Commission on HIV and the Law called for nations to "repeal laws that prohibit consenting adults to buy or sell sex" and that ban "immoral earnings" and brothel-keeping. The U.N. commission also demanded measures "to ensure safe conditions for sex workers." In 2016, Amnesty International— the world's largest human-rights organization — recommended that governments decriminalize consensual sex work and enact laws by which the sex workers are "protected from harm, exploitation and coercion."

In light of the stances by these two global organizations, my campaign to spread the Nevada model for legal prostitution clearly is on the side of history. The time is ripe in America. In 2023, lawmakers in the Vermont Legislature were considering a bill to legalize adult prostitution. Bills to decriminalize prostitution were being considered in New York State Legislature committees.

Bella-style brothels can 'evolutionize' the 'sensual-services' industry

IN MY 38th YEAR as proprietor of a legal brothel, I propose a set of standards that will make the system even safer and saner— serving as a model for the world. I envision the United States and nations around the globe adopting sensible and humane laws regarding sex-for-sale, and societies intelligently shifting their outdated perceptions. In sum, I want to help boost the sex-for-sale industry into the 21st century.

Toward this end, the popular language used for this profession needs to change. This includes embracing a new term for the trade.

The tainted term "prostitution" must be replaced with a dignified designation: "sensual services."

"Prostitute" derives from the Latin *prostitut*, which comes from the Latin verb *prostituere:* to expose publicly or offer for sale. (In Latin, the prefix *pro* means "for" or "before"; *statuo* means "to set up" or "to erect.") The verb — used in the sense of "to offer for indiscriminate sexual intercourse (usually in exchange for money)" — gained usage in English in the 1520s, while the noun was popularized in the 1610s, according to the *Online Etymology Dictionary*. The author of that dictionary's entry added this note in regard to the verb: "The notion of 'sex-for-sale' is not inherent in the etymology, which rather suggests one 'exposed to lust' or sex 'indiscriminately offered.' However, this is now almost the official European term for the institution."

This explanation illustrates how "prostitute" and "prostitution" are unsavory words. They convey lewdness. Say them out loud. How do they make you feel? They sound dirty and derisive, don't they?

The *Merriam-Webster* dictionary presents this primary definition of the noun "prostitute": "a person who engages in sexual intercourse in exchange for pay." The secondary definition: "a person (such as a writer or painter) who deliberately debases his or her talents (as for money)." And here's the secondary definition from *Merriam-Webster* of the transitive verb form of *prostitute*: "to devote to corrupt or unworthy purposes: DEBASE (*prostitute* one's talents)."

If American society and those around the world are going to adopt saner laws and policies regarding sex-for-sale — if they are to treat the profession as a worthy, time-tested vocation that should be legal and regulated like any other service occupation — the vocabulary associated with sex-for-sale needs drastic updating.

"Prostitute" as a noun has these synonyms: hooker, hustler, harlot, bawd, tart, strumpet, trollop, whore, ho. Ugly words! They reflect the stigma attached to all forms of the sex-for-sale industry. Fortunately, the language is slowly evolving.

"Sex worker" is one term gaining in popular usage among activists and academicians, as well as those who provide sex-for-sale. "Sex worker" is a broad term that could apply to a variety of workers in the sex industry — including strippers, porn actors and web-cammers. Activists for sex-worker rights are pushing to replace the term "prostitution" with "full-service sex work": a phrase that implies the worker's control and consent. "Full-service sex work" also differentiates this particular occupation from the other forms of sex work.

> 'Prostitute' as a noun has these synonyms: hooker, hustler, harlot, bawd, tart, strumpet, trollop, whore, ho. Ugly words! They reflect the stigma attached to all forms of the sex-for-sale industry. Fortunately, the language is slowly evolving. 'Sex worker' is gaining popular usage. I favor 'sensual services.'

I find that "full-service sex work" doesn't adequately describe the services offered by the independent contractors at Nevada brothels. Many of their "parties" (sessions) with clients don't even involve sexual intercourse. As for the parties that do, a wide variety of activities are on the menu to satisfy clients' fantasies and fetishes. As detailed in the stories that sex workers at Bella's Hacienda Ranch shared in Chapter Five of this book, a party can involve play acting, sex toys, tutorials, bondage — or even simple cuddling and/or chitchat.

This is why I favor the term "sensual services" instead of "sex work." It is more accurate, more evocative of the services offered, and more respectable. It has a pretty ring to it, too: *Sensual services.*

"Sensual" derives from the Latin *sensualis*, meaning, "endowed with feeling." In English — according to *Merriam-Webster* — it primarily means "relating to or consisting in the gratification of the senses or the indulgence of appetite."

There is nothing inherently unseemly about this very human need for fulfillment, is there?

As for "sex worker," I prefer a more elegant term for the women who capably provide sensual services in the legal setting of a brothel: *courtesan*.

"Courtesan" needs to be adopted as the word used for the skilled women who provide sensual services in legal brothels.

"Courtesan" is comparable to a master in a trade, as opposed to a journeyman or apprentice. The word reflects capability, professionalism and devotion to one's line of work. In Chapter Three I cited Veronica Franco — an admired and accomplished, self-sufficient courtesan in 16th century Venice — as an example of a woman who elevated the providing of sensual services to its highest level in her society. Franco attained a status akin to that of a noblewoman. She was a member of an upper stratum of sex worker: a *cortigiana onesta* — "honored courtesan."

The Italian word *cortigiana* literally means "woman of the court," yet it came to be used, euphemistically or mockingly, to refer to a woman who provided sex to an upper-class or wealthy clientele. In English, "courtesan" came to be yet another synonym for prostitute, although it didn't carry the same derogatory sense as prostitute or its pejoratives, such as "whore."

"Courtesan" has a dignified ring. Say it out loud. Don't you agree? Imagine, in the not-to-distant future, when a person patronizing a legal brothel goes there to pursue sensual services from a courtesan, rather than sex from a prostitute. Words carry enormous weight. Vocabularies shape our thinking, our perception of reality.

This is why my campaign to "evolutionize" (a word I've coined) the sensual-services industry includes the push to replace the word "prostitution" with "sensual services," and "prostitute" with "courtesan." I aim for these language changes to be made in Nevada's statutes, as well. When the laws themselves refer to a profession in respectful terms, the entire legal system will experience a shift toward fairness and humaneness for that profession.

Evolutionizing the industry through empowerment

MY MISSION AS MADAM Bella is to "evolutionize" the sensual-services industry. One of my key objectives is to make it possible for courtesans to work in a nurturing environment — one that facilitates them meeting their financial goals. Some courtesans may want to work in the profession only temporarily; others may want to make a career of it.

Here is one of my core beliefs:

Providing sensual services should allow each courtesan a route to economic independence and personal empowerment.

This is especially important for women — who, historically, have been hard-pressed to support themselves, much less grow wealthy working for themselves in a male-dominated world.

Bella's Hacienda Ranch is one of the few legal brothels owned and operated by a woman. I and the independent contractors who come to work for me pursue female empowerment *together*. You can read how this works in the experiences that Tandy, Lacey and other courtesans at Bella's explained in Chapter Five. Tandy, for example, described how I encourage the women to set goals for themselves to attract prosperity into their lives. This manifesting includes writing empowerment statements on the white board in the kitchen. Tandy also related how this positive energy feeds on itself in a spirit of sisterhood:

"Bella says, 'Empowered women empower women.' I'd never experienced anything like it."

Lacey also embraced my preaching about female empowerment:

"It's knowing we have the ability and the choice to do exactly what we want to do and manifest what we desire in our lives. Being empowered is us knowing that, and using whatever ability we have to get where we need to in life, and become more of who we came to be in the second decade of a feminine millennium."

I promote collective female empowerment at Bella's Hacienda. I guide the women to attain the level of *courtesanship*. Courtesanship means providing sensual services to achieve one's own financial aims and self-sufficiency, and providing those services as an esteemed calling. It means giving customers the soul-nourishing touch, warmth and attention they are so desperately in need of, and are so willing to pay for.

In the end, providing sensual services at the courtesan level can have profound effects for society as a whole. We live in an age rife with mass alienation. Rates of depression, addiction, and suicide are on the rise. Road rage remains a problem. Social-media sites roil with hostile posts from bitter trolls. The evidence is all around us of frustrated, despairing individuals whose own humanity is compromised by a lack of intimate human contact. The way I phrase it is they lack — or have lost — the ability to comprehend how to be human correctly: to appreciate each day for its blessings, to enjoy the company of others, to feel empathy for strangers.

One of the strongest arguments for legalizing and regulating sensual services —— instead of leaving sex-for-sale in the shadows, further straining over-stretched criminal-justice systems and creating health hazards — is that it can have a powerful *humanizing* effect. It can contribute to the psychological welfare of society.

If sensual services are legally offered in Nevada-style brothels and located where they can be conveniently reached by the general adult population across this nation, and globe, they no longer would be inaccessible or unattractive to lonely, needy or disheartened souls who could benefit tremendously from courtesan-level sensual services.

Life would be better for them, and for the rest of society.

A deterrent to incel violence?

WHEN I SEE NEWS stories about a troubled and frustrated young man committing wanton violence against random strangers, I can't help but wonder whether the crime could have been avoided had the perpetrator assuaged his anger and sorrow through seeking professional sensual services. This is only speculation. Mental health is extremely

CHAPTER FOUR

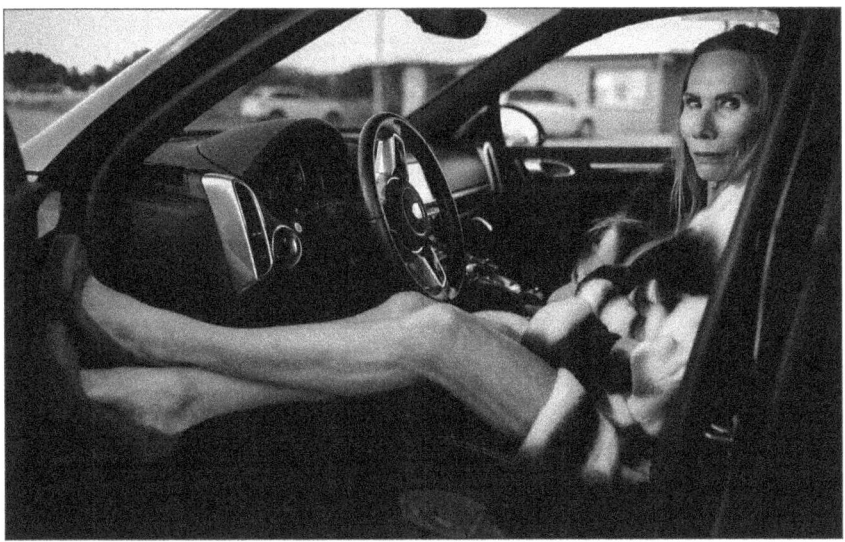

A madam's work keeps her on the go. *Photo by Victory Tischler-Blue*

complex. There is no panacea — not even psychotherapy or antidepressants — for curing every form of severe psychological problem.

Consider the following story, however, which gained national headlines:

On April 12, 2019, a mother and her son at the Mall of America in Minneapolis were approached by a 24-year-old man. The stranger seized the boy and threw him over the railing of the three-story balcony. Miraculously, the boy survived landing on the concrete floor 39 feet below. Paramedics revived him and rushed him to a hospital.

The man was quickly arrested. He told police investigators he'd visited the mall for years attempting to pick up women, and the constant rejection made him lash out. He said he'd gone to the mall that day planning on killing an adult, then chose the child instead.

It turned out the man had been convicted twice before for assaults at the mall and been banned from the property. At his sentencings for those incidents, he'd been ordered to undergo psychological evaluation or treatment. At his sentencing hearing on the balcony incident, he told the judge that he'd completed the required treatment for the previous assaults.

The man pleaded guilty to attempted premeditated murder and was sentenced that June to 19 years in prison. (As for the boy, following multiple surgeries and other care over four-and-a-half months, he returned home.)

There are even more chilling news stories — centered on infuriated, frustrated men — capturing headlines these days: stories of mass shootings. Statistics are grim. In 2019, there were 417 mass shootings in the nation: more than in any year since a nonprofit organization, the Gun Violence Archive, began keeping such records in 2014. The GVA defines a "mass shooting" as any incident in which four or more people are shot, not including the shooter.

Some experts say the shooters — nearly all of them men — are driven by rage over perceived wrongs to themselves, even if a shooter ascribes his violence to some political, social or religious ideology or cause. "At its core, it's all really personal," Adam Lankford, a University of Alabama professor of criminology, told *USA Today* reporters. Lankford's comments were solicited by journalists after a week in summer 2019 in which a 21-year-old man (who espoused anti-immigrant beliefs) shot dead 22 people and injured 24 others at a Walmart store in El Paso, Texas; a 24-year-old man (whom authorities said held misogynist views) shot dead nine people and wounded 16 others at a popular bar in Dayton, Ohio; and a 19-year-old man (whose home and computer contained left-wing and right-wing literature) shot three dead and injured at least a dozen more at a garlic festival in Gilroy, California.

Professor Lankford said mass shooters share a mindset referred to as an "injustice collector." Even if they claim to be motivated to kill because of attacks by perceived enemies against their gender, race or religion — "latching on to some anger that's bigger than them" — they often feel they've been personally wronged, mistreated or ignored.

How do mass shootings tie into sexual deprivation?

Although it is only conjecture, it is obvious to me that sexual deprivation lies at the root of many or most of these crimes. Consider that so-called "incels" — a word coined from the phrase "involuntary celibates" — have been culprits or suspects in several mass murders and other violent attacks in America. A well-sourced *Wikipedia* article on this subject explains that incels "are members of an online subculture who define themselves as unable to find a romantic or sexual partner despite desiring one, a state they describe as inceldom." The *Wikipedia* article lists the following attacks attributed to or suspected to have been committed by men claiming to identify as incels, or who have mentioned incel-related writings or names in their own private writings or online posts. The attacks (and threatened attacks) include these:

- On May 23, 2014, 22-year-old Elliot Rodger — whose fury over being rejected by women had led to a reported string of incidents in preceding years, including tossing coffee on a couple he followed out of a Starbucks, splashing coffee on two girls sitting at a bus stop who didn't smile back at him, and attempting to shove girls over a 10-foot ledge at a party after they mocked him — went on a rampage. He stabbed his two roommates and a visitor to death, apparently one by one as they arrived at his apartment. Next, he shot three women outside a sorority house at the University of California, Santa Barbara (two died). Then he shot to death a male student at a nearby deli. Then he sped his car through the town of Isla Vista, shooting and wounding pedestrians and striking others with his car. He exchanged gunfire with police before crashing his car into a parked vehicle. Before he could be arrested, he fatally shot himself in the head. His final toll was six murdered, 14 injured, and his own suicide.

  Of special note is that after stabbing the three men in his apartment and before driving to the sorority house, Rodger uploaded to YouTube a video he titled, "Elliot Rodger's Retribution." The video outlined his upcoming attack and explained it was to punish women for rejecting him, and punish sexually active men because he envied them. Rodger then emailed to several acquaintances, relatives and his therapist a document he titled, "My Twisted World: The Story of Elliot Rodger." It circulated on the Internet and became known as Rodger's manifesto.

- On Oct. 1, 2015, 26-year-old Chris Harper-Mercer shot to death nine people and injured eight more before killing himself in a classroom at Umpqua Community College in Roseburg, Oregon. Harper-Mercer left a manifesto at the scene describing his anger at not having a girlfriend and proclaiming his interest in Rodger's and other mass murders.
- On Dec. 7, 2017, 21-year-old William Atchison, a high school dropout, shot to death a cheerleader and a football player at his former school, Aztec High School, before killing himself. Atchison had used the pseudonym "Elliot Rodger" on online forums.
- On Valentine's Day, 2018, 19-year-old Nikolas Cruz shot to death 17 students and teachers and wounded 17 others at Marjory Stoneman Douglas High School in Parkland, Florida. Cruz had posted, "Elliot Rodger will not be forgotten" in a YouTube comment.
- On April 23, 2018, 25-year-old Alex Minassian killed 10 pedestrians and injured 16 others by ramming them with a rented van he drove through streets in Toronto. Investigators later found a Facebook post from Minassian in which he identified himself as an incel. The post said: "The Incel Rebellion has already begun! We will overthrow all the Chads and Stacys! All hail the Supreme Gentleman Elliot Rodger! ("Chad" and "Stacy" are terms used on incel-related web forums to refer to attractive, sexually active men and women.)
- On Jan. 19, 2019, 27-year-old Christopher Wayne Cleary was arrested by FBI agents and police in Provo, Utah, after posting on Facebook about his "planning on shooting up a public place soon and being the next mass shooter," and "killing as many girls as I see" because he was a virgin and had never had a girlfriend. At the time of his arrest, Cleary, of Denver, was serving probation for stalking a woman. Eight women and female teens in the Denver area had reported to police that Cleary had harassed them when they wouldn't date them.
- On June 17, 2019, 22-year-old Bryan Isaack Clyde began shooting up the Earl Cabell Federal Building and Courthouse in Dallas, armed with a rifle and more than 150 rounds of ammunition. Fortunately,

officers from the Federal Protective Service shot and fatally wounded Clyde before he could hit anyone. Clyde — who'd been honorably discharged from the U.S. Army after a two-year stint (during which he hadn't been deployed) — had posted incel memes on his social-media accounts, as well as memes about the Confederate States and Nazism.

Violence from incels isn't restricted to sex-starved men in their teens or twenties.

- On July 31, 2016, 38-year-old security guard Sheldon Russell Bentley was summoned by a fellow guard at a strip mall in Toronto to wake up a man passed out in the alley. Bentley stomped his combat boot into the man's torso, rupturing the abdomen and causing fatal internal bleeding.

  The psychiatrist and probation officer who submitted reports to the court at Bentley's sentencing (he was convicted of manslaughter) said Bentley was angry and frustrated about his inability to find a sexual partner. The probation officer wrote that Bentley told her of his failed efforts to attract a girlfriend in person or online, and that his only romantic relationship had been when he was 27. "He indicated it was the happiest time of his life, as he had his first sexual experience and felt loved," the parole officer wrote, adding, "During the time of the offence, the subject spoke to how he had built up stress from not having any sexual relations."

- On Nov. 2, 2018, 30-year-old Scott Beierle — a military veteran and former schoolteacher — fatally shot two women, wounded four others and pistol-whipped a man at a yoga studio in Tallahassee, Florida, before killing himself. Beierle had been fired as a substitute teacher at one school after asking a female student if she was ticklish and then touching her on her stomach. He'd also been charged twice for battery, accused each time of grabbing a woman's buttocks. Beierle posted YouTube videos of himself expressing deep hatred for women and his anger over not having a girlfriend. Not surprisingly, he said he identified with the incel community and sympathized with Elliot Rodger.

Would the Elliot Rodgers of the world be drawn out of their incel rage by patronizing a safe and comforting legal brothel?

This is such a controversial topic that I wonder if any bona fide researchers would care to put together a study to shed much-needed light on it. If any researchers *were* seriously interested, perhaps they could measure the boosts in mood and confidence of frustrated men after receiving sensual services by a professional courtesan at a legal brothel. The researchers could compare the men's emotional states before and after. They also could compare the results to that of control groups — for example, men who aren't sexually frustrated yet visit brothels, men who are in romantic relationships who don't visit brothels, and so on.

Comedian and political commentator Bill Maher broadened the argument that sexual frustration is the source of deadly mass violence to include more than incels as culprits. On an Oct. 16, 2015, episode of his *HBO* talk show *Real Time With Bill Maher*, he linked the root cause of the Chris Harper-Mercer shooting spree earlier that month with that of Elliot Rodger the previous year — *and* with the 2007 rampage by a 23-year-old college student at Virginia Tech who shot to death 32 people and wounded 17 others, the 2012 shooting by a 20-year-old man at Sandy Hook Elementary School in Connecticut, and the 1995 bombing of the federal building in Oklahoma City by 33-year-old Timothy McVeigh, which killed 168 people and injured more than 680 others: the deadliest act of domestic terrorism in the United States.

"Timothy McVeigh famously never had a date and almost certainly died a virgin," Maher said. "I don't know for a fact that no man in history has ever said: 'Sex, sex, sex, that's all I ever do! Where's my gun?! I'm mad at the world!' I just know it's true."

Maher continued: "We need to wake up and smell the testosterone. The reason behind so many of these tragedies has been right in our face. Throbbing. Angrily. And if you think young men in America are throbbing angrily, what would you estimate the sexual frustration level to be for a young man who grows up only ever seeing women who look like this or this?"

The studio screen flashed images of women in a conservative Muslim nation shrouded head to toe in burqas that even concealed their faces. That was the wind-up to Maher's punchline:

"How do you even masturbate to that? I know masturbation requires imagination but that's ridiculous!"

Of course, the subject is no laughing matter. After the Bryan Isaack Clyde shooting at the federal building in Dallas, officers at the Joint Base Andrews-Naval Air Facility Washington, in Maryland, initiated a program that teaches personnel to recognize the warning signs that "introverted, sexless individuals" may be attracted to the incel online subculture. A base spokesman described incels as "a very real threat to military members and civilians."

A report in January 2020 by the Texas Department of Public Safety cautioned that incels are an "emerging domestic terrorism threat."

This sense of foreboding already was invoked by Stephen T. Asma, a philosophy professor at Columbia College Chicago who has authored several books on the human mind. Asma penned an essay, published in June 2016 on *Aeon.com*, titled, "The Weaponised Loser." Asma wrote: "The shooter is socially alienated, and he can't get laid. Every time you scratch the surface of the latest mass killing, in a movie theatre, a school, the streets of Paris or an abortion clinic, you find the weaponised loser. From Jihadi John of ISIS to Dylan Klebold and Eric Harris at Columbine, these men are invariably stuck in the emotional life of an adolescent. They always struggle with self-esteem — especially regarding women — and sometimes they give up entirely on the possibility of amorous fulfilment."

Asma argued that it's time to examine the possibility of causes of terrorism beyond religious fervor, political beliefs or economic causes. He wrote: "Freudian interpretations of the news might be out of style, but we would do well to revitalise them." Asma also warned that sexually frustrated men can't simply be deterred from violent urges by talking to them:

"Male desire and craving are not intellectualised away with some didactic lecture about how the brain or the economy works, or some sermon about what Jesus or Muhammad want from you. Desire must be redirected into some form of non-destructive expression, or defused, not just talked about. It's the job of culture to help with this redirection, and the Abrahamic cultural traditions have outlived their effectiveness in doing so. We need to get working on some new cultural inventions to domesticate resentment and the hydraulics of hate, or the growing pack of weaponised losers will make political terrorism look tame by comparison."

'Hollywood Madam' Heidi Fleiss wrote in an op-ed piece that sexual services have always been in demand, and making transactional sex illegal creates a bigger black market.

As a "new cultural invention," I modestly propose making legal brothels widely accessible and acceptable in society. They would provide incels a safe and clean place in which to "domesticate" their resentment and "hydraulics of hate."

There may be no better solution to this deadly problem!

Safe havens from violence, disease, arrest, trafficking

WHEN I SAY LEGAL brothels are "safe and clean," I can't emphasize enough the advantage of patronizing a Nevada-style legal brothel rather than an illegal venue for sex-for-sale.

In a legal Nevada brothel, there is no risk of a guest being assaulted by a pimp — or rolled by a sex worker, his wallet stolen, or worse. And the risk of contracting a sexually transmitted disease or infection is — as previously mentioned — near zero. It's worth mentioning here that the rates of new gonorrhea, chlamydia and syphilis cases in the United States rose for a fifth straight year in 2019, according to a report from the U.S. Centers for Disease Control and Prevention. This should alarm anyone who patronizes an illegal venue or operator for sex. Let's remember that, unlike legal sex workers, illegal sex workers — including high-priced call girls and escorts — don't face losing their livelihood if they fail to undergo regular and thorough testing for sexually transmitted diseases or infections. They work outside the law, not needing work cards and background checks before servicing clients.

Of course, the "safe and clean" aspects of legal brothels are equally advantageous to the sex workers themselves. As noted previously in this chapter, sex workers are vulnerable to violence when working illegally. One tragic fact that's unpleasant to broach, yet germane to the subject of safety, is that serial killers are prone to target prostitutes. As James Alan Fox, a criminology professor and co-author of the book *Extreme Killing*, wrote in an Oct. 23, 2014, column in *USA Today*: "Serial murders of prostitutes — streetwalkers, escorts, and outcall sex workers — have occurred in virtually every state of the nation, with many of the cases unsolved and frustratingly cold." Fox went on to cite research by criminal-justice professor Kenna Quinet that shows "as many as one-third of repeat killers have included prostitutes among their prey."

Legal brothels are safe zones for courtesans. They maintain their anonymity and privacy while plying their trade in a secure environment. And they work without the constant stress of being arrested — an anxiety illegal sex workers have in common with their clients. In a legal brothel, the patrons need not fret about being busted, prosecuted and humiliated simply for paying for sex. This surely is a great relief.

Every so often, the arrest of a famous and powerful man for soliciting sex grabs world headlines. In a case fraught with irony, then-New York Gov. Elliot Spitzer resigned from office in 2008 after news broke that he had patronized an international escort agency, the Emperors Club VIP, which turned out to be a high-priced prostitution ring. Federal investigators, alerted by suspiciously large money transfers from Gov. Spitzer's bank account, had wiretapped his phone. Thus ended the career of a rising star whom political pundits had speculated could have made a strong run for the White House. The irony was that when Spitzer was a hard-charging New York state attorney general — building up his stock to run for governor — he'd prosecuted several prostitution rings.

More recently, Robert Kraft, owner of the NFL's New England Patriots, was arrested on charges of soliciting prostitution in Jupiter, Florida, in February 2019. The arrest in a multi-city sting of massage parlors came a few weeks after the Patriots had won their sixth Super Bowl. Kraft pleaded not guilty to the charges stemming from his alleged paying for sex at the Orchids of Asia Day Spa in the south Florida city the previous month. Police investigators claimed Kraft was caught on their surveillance video receiving a sex act with a spa worker on two separate days. If convicted, he faced up to a year in prison, a $5,000 fine, 100 hours of community service and mandatory attendance at a class on the dangers of prostitution and human trafficking. Why would the class curriculum include "human trafficking"? Prosecutors alleged that managers of the day spas under surveillance were sex trafficking women, forcing them to perform sex acts on clients.

The Patriots owner's arrest and the subject of trafficking spurred a wonderful opinion piece, published in *USA Today*, written by Heidi Fleiss and titled, "Want to Stop Human Trafficking? Legalize Consensual Sex for Money." In case her name is unfamiliar to you, Fleiss gained notoriety in the 1990s as the twentysomething, so-called "Hollywood Madam" who'd been arrested for running an upscale sex ring in Los Angeles that catered to rich and prominent clients.

In her op-ed piece in *USA Today*, Fleiss explained why someone rich and powerful like Kraft "who likely has women throwing themselves at him on a daily basis" would go to a massage parlor for sex. Her answer was simple: "Because he wanted to. It was there. Sometimes you want to eat a nice steak, and sometimes you want fast food. It was the fast-food equivalent of sex."

The only problems with Kraft's alleged visit to the spa for sex, Fleiss wrote, were: "It happens to be illegal; the women there were reportedly victims of sex trafficking; the two points above are closely linked." She continued: "There's a problem that has led to this problem. We are a society tied in knots around sexuality and sexual pleasure. We all love it, but we have such specific, archaic rules around where and when we are allowed to feel it. If we had the same rules around happiness, there would be a revolution."

Fleiss asserted that sexual services have always been in demand, and making "transactional sex" illegal simply creates a bigger black market for it. Conversely, legalizing prostitution can reduce sex trafficking, she wrote. "New Zealand legalized prostitution in 2003. In a 2008 study, the New Zealand Ministry of Justice found no incidence of trafficking over the previous five years. Sex worker advocates also say the law made it easier for them to report abuse, and for law enforcement to make arrests for crimes committed against sex workers."

Sex trafficking is an extremely disturbing subject. The news about a federal indictment alleging that the wealthy financier Jeffrey Epstein — whose associates included powerful U.S. businessmen and politicians and international celebrities, including the Duke of York — ran a sex-trafficking ring exploiting dozens of minor girls at his homes in New York, Florida and elsewhere in the early 2000s, made headlines for months. (Epstein's death, reportedly by suicide, in his prison cell in August 2019 spared him prosecution.)

Opponents of prostitution often cite sex trafficking as an evil their efforts are combatting. Unfortunately, their targets include legal brothels. (I mentioned, in Chapter Three, recent efforts by anti-traffickers to ban brothels in two Nevada counties.)

The truth is that the Nevada model of legal brothels is a bulwark against sex trafficking and slavery. In this chapter I've mentioned the research paper, "Sex Industry and Sex Workers in Nevada," published in 2012 by three researchers at the University of Nevada, Las Vegas. The authors noted that the two groups of victims that anti-sex-trafficking advocates are most concerned about are "migrants who may be pulled into a black market for sex that transports foreign nationals through coercion or deceit to the U.S. or other Western countries," and "teenagers lured into prostitution by pimps and third parties."

It is far-fetched to assume migrant and teen-age victims of trafficking wind up in legal brothels in Nevada, where the sex workers must pass criminal-background checks by the local sheriff's office, and where they work in an environment in which they can seek help from peers or police.

Breanna Mohr — who worked in a Nevada brothel while attending college, and co-authored with two professors the previously cited book *Sex and Stigma: Stories of Everyday Life in Nevada's Legal Brothels* — recalled putting in volunteer hours in a community organization as a semester project in graduate school. Mohr chose a local anti-sex trafficking organization. She wrote: "This organization claims that 81 percent of working girls in the brothels want to 'escape.' I have worked alongside women in the brothels for roughly four full years, and I can say that's just not true."

Earlier in this section, I shared key points from a master's thesis, "The Viability of Nevada's Legal Brothels as Models for Regulation and Harm Reduction in Prostitution," written by David H. Rodgers, a criminal-justice graduate student at Florida State University in 2010. In his thesis, Rodgers cited the work of UNLV sociology professors Barbara G. Brents and Kathryn Hausbeck, who interviewed sex workers in Nevada brothels about their work experiences, and included their responses in a chapter of the book, *Sex for Sale: Prostitution, Pornography, and the Sex Industry*, published in 2010. Rodgers wrote:

"All of the prostitutes interviewed by Hausbeck and Brents (2010) reported that they were working in brothels as a matter of voluntary choice, and none reported being trafficked or knowing of anyone else who had been trafficked. Although they were not directly questioned about pimps, few mentioned them, and some said they had fled to the brothels to get away from them. Further, the point was made that the brothel owners themselves depend on being able to provide a safe and acceptable alternative to illegal prostitution in order to survive, thus providing common goals from ethical and economic interests."

Once again, I make this point:

Imagine if legal brothels — staffed by independent contractors with work cards issued after an extensive criminal background check, and who submit to regular medical examinations to ensure they are free of STDs — were accessible to the customers who currently resort to patronizing illegal venues for sensual services. There wouldn't be arrest and prosecution of the likes of Robert Kraft and Elliot Spitzer, or the great many other ordinary, non-famous, non-wealthy souls whose only crime is seeking intimate pleasure and companionship, and agreeing to pay money for it.

After Spitzer's resignation from office, University of Chicago law professor Martha Nussbaum wrote in an opinion piece in the *Atlanta Journal-Constitution* newspaper: "Eliot Spitzer, one of the nation's most gifted and dedicated politicians, was hounded into resignation by a Puritanism and mean-spiritedness that are quintessentially American. . . . In Germany and the Netherlands, prostitution is legal and regulated by public health authorities. A man who did what Spitzer did would have a lot to discuss with his wife and family, but he would have broken no laws, and it would be laughable to accuse him of a betrayal of the public trust. This is as it should be. If Spitzer broke any laws, they were bad laws, laws that should never have existed."

Let's hope these laws will cease to exist after sexual evolution takes place.

CHAPTER FIVE

Courtesans' Stories — in Their Own Words

In summer 2019, I invited the women in residence at Bella's Hacienda to share with an interviewer their experiences and opinions about the sensual-services industry. Some were happy to oblige; others demurred, concerned about protecting their privacy, even though their real names and other identifying details would be left out. I could appreciate their reluctance. The greatest stressor for many women who work in sensual services is their struggle to conceal their work from family, friends and the public. Their anxiety has to do with the stigma society places on sex work.

Women from many different backgrounds, with widely differing personal characteristics, constitute the independent contractors who work in brothels. One of the women who's worked for me is European born, cultured, fluent in multiple languages and boasts a university graduate degree. The sky-high costs of medical care in the United States compelled her to come to Bella's to stave off debt. Another woman — an Asian native who is well traveled and speaks several languages — had worked for escort services and was drawn to Bella's for the safety of working in a legal brothel. Seared into her memory is the traumatic episode when a customer in a major East Coast city held a knife to her throat. She'd extricated herself using a survival-mode mix of wrestling and verbal skills (the latter involving the grisly picture she painted for him of the retribution he'd suffer at the hands of mobsters who ran the escort service.)

Again, not every courtesan I approached was open to being interviewed. Of those who were, their insights into this ancient profession, in its modern incarnation in a legal Nevada brothel, will be informative to anyone with a serious and sincere interest in this industry — and in human sexuality, in general.

* * *

Tandy: Giant passion in a little body

Tandy stands all of 5-foot-4 in her heels, and weighs a yoga-lean 115 pounds, yet she's a powerhouse in her trade. Her libido is prodigious. She oozes sex appeal in or out of the schoolgirl-next-door outfit she sports for lineups.

Her online profile proclaims, "I am your total GFE fantasy" — and if that fantasy of a "girlfriend experience" includes blond hair, a clear-complexioned face with a high forehead and big brown eyes, a 34-22-30 figure, a high, soft girlish voice prone to ready giggles, and a tender, nurturing touch that is comforting and exciting at the same time, then Tandy is your wet dream in the flesh.

It's no surprise that Tandy's usually the most popular pick in the lineups. She stands out like a fresh flower with its petals parted in bloom.

In truth, Tandy is a late bloomer in the brothel business. She didn't enter the profession until she was on the late side of her thirties.

A series of life changes propelled Tandy into this field she hadn't known existed before she relocated to Nevada after a divorce.

TANDY GREW UP IN the Seattle area. The fourth of five children in a middle-class home, she became pregnant in high school and become a mother at 16. At 18, she married the father of her child. After they divorced, she married a wealthy man who provided her and her young son a life of leisure. They lived in Olympia, the capital of Washington state.

Before this marriage, Tandy had earned an associate's degree in communications, and found a decent-paying job in medical billing. The wealth from her marriage, though, precluded her need to continue earning an income. She'd focused on raising her son and enjoying the good life.

The marriage broke up after Tandy realized her husband had a serious drinking problem and she couldn't do anything to get him to change course. She herself didn't drink, even socially, "so it was a huge problem," she explained. "My husband would 'disappear' at a certain time of the night. He was there in the house, but he wasn't the same person."

After her divorce, Tandy received spousal support yet had to readjust to living beneath the means to which she'd grown accustomed. "My ex-husband had amassed most of the wealth before we were married. I didn't get half the estate. I did get a good divorce settlement, though."

Craving a change of surroundings to recover from the divorce, Tandy moved 1,000 miles away, to Las Vegas, where her now-adult son lived. She came up with a plan to live in style: She'd rent a big, expensive house in the Vegas suburb of Henderson, then become an Airbnb hostess — renting out rooms or the entire house to guests for periods of time. This would allow her to cover her rent and still live in style.

"It was very successful for a couple of months," Tandy said. "It was constantly booked, and I loved hosting. I was having a really good time."

Then the good people of the home-owners association put an end to it.

"They didn't like the short-term rental, transient situation. I had to shut that down. Now I was in this lease for an insane amount of rent, and it was taking most of my spousal support. I was spending beyond my means. And I'm thinking, 'What am I going to do?'"

She realized that Nevada, the state in which she now resided, had legal brothels. They piqued her curiosity.

"I've always been interested in the sex industry," Tandy said. "When

I was in school, my papers for psychology and sociology classes would always be geared to the sex industry. It was always intriguing to me, for some reason. It was kind of a natural thought process for me, when things started to break down in Las Vegas, to do some research on the brothels in Nevada."

Brothels in the Silver State are legal only in rural counties whose governments approve them. State law prohibits brothels in counties above a certain population. Clark County, home to Las Vegas and Henderson, is the most populous of Nevada's 17 counties, and brothels are not permitted there. The closest legal brothels to where Tandy was living were in the Nye County town of Pahrump, 70 miles away. One was the Chicken Ranch. Tandy applied to work there via an online form, attaching her photo. She also applied to the state's most famous brothel: the Moonlite BunnyRanch, in Mound House, just east of the state capital of Carson City, 450 miles north.

"They did over-the-phone interviews, and I was accepted to both houses, but I chickened out," Tandy said. "I kept saying, 'I'll get back to you with a date,' but I didn't ever call and set a date."

She was wracked with fears and doubt. *Oh, my God, can I do it? Am I too old? Am I capable of this? Am I qualified? What would it take?*

"I just kept talking myself out of it. And meanwhile, I'm driving for Uber and Lyft. It was terrible. It was especially hard being a woman driving in Vegas."

Tourists out for a good time viewed a pretty Uber driver as fair game to hit on.

Tandy could have returned to Washington state, where her large family lived, and where she could have gotten support to resettle herself. She could have returned to working in medical billing. However, she wasn't emotionally ready to head back to her former environs. She had made a clean break so she could work through the emotional aftermath of her divorce. She wanted to stick it out in Nevada.

"Something was driving me to explore my independence," she said.

CHAPTER FIVE

TANDY CONTINUED RESEARCHING BROTHELS.

"One day, I was visiting Bella's website. For some reason, the working-girl page was not interactive. I ended up calling Bella's. It just so happened that Bella herself picked up the phone. She's not always here, so it was lucky.

"It was a Saturday in November, and I'm signed on for Uber that day. I'm waiting for a ride to bid on, and I'm on the phone with the owner of this brothel. I'll never forget this. It wasn't frightening. Her demeanor, her tone, were accepting and warm. We chatted for what must have been forty-five minutes. She was incredibly easy to talk to.

"She asked if I had ever done this kind of work before. She asked where I was located. Mostly, she just explained to me the process, how the house worked. I shared with her my age, thinking that

Tandy. *Photo property of Bella Cummins*

would be an issue, and she just reassured me that it's not age, it's *you*. It's what *you* have to offer the world. It's not about a stereotype. She said that if *you* are confident, if *you* think that you can offer something and be of service to people, and are warm and open to that, then you'll do really well.

"She wasn't intending to convince me to come, or convince me not to. She was just being informative. It was completely woman to woman. The whole thing that she talks about is *female empowerment*. She made me feel like we would empower each other. The managers at the other two brothels I'd interacted with on the phone were women, but the conversations were strictly about business. They weren't personal."

I remember this phone call well. As Tandy and I chatted, I not only allayed her fears about flopping as a sex worker because of her lack of experience and her age, I evidently inspired her to give it a shot by explaining the show-business aspect of the profession. In Tandy's words:

"What she said to me was, 'You're still who you are, but you get to transform into anyone you want to be. Don't be limited by who've you been all your life — whether it's Suzie Homemaker, or what have you — because here you can be Marilyn Monroe if you want to be. Or you can come here and wear a tiara.'

"It sounded fun! It didn't matter that I'd been a wife and mom my whole adult life. I could bring my passion, my heart, my ways with me, and still transform into another woman that would be suitable for this industry.

"It was a really empowering conversation! And actually, that very day, I finally committed to a starting date. We agreed that I'd show up the coming Wednesday, which was five days away. I'd start on Friday and be up there for two weeks.

"Honestly, I didn't even know if I'd make it a week!"

I HAD EXPLAINED TO Tandy that she would stay in a room at my brothel, and that on Thursday morning — the morning after her arrival — she'd have her doctor's examination in Wells. Upon receiving medical clearance, she would proceed to the sheriff's department for fingerprinting and a background check. Assuming she had no criminal record that would prevent her from working at the brothel, she'd get her work card that day and be available to start at Bella's right away.

Tandy set out from Henderson early that Wednesday morning. On the 400-mile, seven-hour drive up U.S. 93, she pulled over three times to calm herself down. She told herself: *Breathe, breathe. You can do this.*

Tandy finally reached Wells. She found the turnoff from U.S. 93 onto the unpaved Hacienda Ranch Road, winded up the half-mile through the sagebrush and dirt and came upon the lot with Donna's and Bella's. Neither single-story structure looked anything in the way of elegant to her. Donna's was an A-frame house with single-wide trailers stuck to it. There was cheap roofing on top and a latticed fence in front like some tawdry back-country roadhouse. A white wood sign attached to the fence spelled out in red letters: "World Famous DONNA's Ranch." A red arrow beneath pointed to the entrance.

Just tacky, to Tandy's eyes.

At least Bella's looked much better to her, although it's certainly no glitzy resort. Bella's Hacienda is a single-story stucco building the color of cinnamon, with a wing coming off to form an L. A big sign on two poles standing in front reads, "BELLA's" in big black letters over a magenta background.

Tandy remembered: "I thought, 'My gosh. What did I get myself into?'" Well, there was no turning back now.

"I parked. I rang the doorbell. I was greeted by one of the bartenders, Tina, with a huge hug. She knew I was coming. She walked me through the house. Bella had left the house a few days after we'd talked on the phone, and wasn't due to be back for some time.

"I was really, really nervous. I was able to pick out the room I wanted. There were only a couple left."

Tandy chose the room at the end of the new wing.

"I've been here ever since," she said. "It's been good to me."

BY THE FOLLOWING AFTERNOON she'd passed her medical examination and applied for her work card at the Elko County Sheriff's substation, in Wells. Now she needed a fair number of pointers on how to prepare for working as a courtesan at Bella's Hacienda Ranch. The list was lengthy, indeed. She'd need the right clothes, the right supplies. She'd need to know how the system of lineups, negotiations and payment worked, and how to check a customer for signs of sexually transmitted

Three courtesans model their lingerie by the bar.
Photo by Brandi Betancourt

infection before the party could start. She'd need to know what was permitted in a party and the procedures for ending a party.

The butterflies flapping in her belly were not just from the strange environment she found herself in. They also were from the realization she soon would be taking the plunge into having sex with strangers for money. The butterflies also were from her concerns how she — a total rookie — would fit in. She was, after all, in a house with seven other women also grinding out a living.

"I was thinking that the women would be catty. That they wouldn't want the success of another girl. That they wouldn't be welcoming."

Her anxiety was quickly assuaged. Tandy was paired with a "big sister" to orient and support her on her first night. This mentor was a pretty young woman from Arizona of mixed white and Asian ancestry. She had the room next to Tandy's and went by the name Mercedes. She was 22, a year younger than Tandy's son, yet in the house she was Tandy's senior. And she took her training seriously.

Mercedes turned out to be kind, friendly and helpful. Tandy's relief was immense.

"This environment that Bella's set up is for women empowerment," Tandy said. "Bella says, 'Empowered women empower women.' I'd never experienced anything like it."

Tandy saw that the women at Bella's shared a teamwork mentality.

I'd instilled the mindset that they were in this campaign together: participating in the oldest profession, carrying on the legacy of the respected courtesans of old. If they supported each other, they would all do better. Because they collaborated as a team to provide excellent service, the men would show up with plenty of money to spread around.

Still, Tandy trembled with first-night jitters.

Mercedes wrote out a little list of the supplies Tandy needed to buy from a store that afternoon: condoms, baby wipes, lubricant, antibacterial soap, medical gloves. Tandy bought them at the Family Dollar, one of the two stores in Wells that sells such items.

"As soon as you walk in, they look at you, and they know why you're in town," Tandy said. "It was humiliating. Looking back, though, maybe it was all in my head, because I already was feeling so self-conscious."

THURSDAY EVENING WAS FAST approaching. Tandy had brought a few outfits with her. She hadn't come up with a special persona yet, so she'd packed what she thought would look enticing: evening dresses, lingerie, elegant jewelry.

She dressed up. Mercedes gave her a pep talk.

"She told me to be confident, not timid. She told me not to let a man talk down to me. She told me to value myself as far as setting my rates, to place a high value on myself. She told me to stick to my guns. She said, 'Tell people about you, and what you offer.'

"She walked me through what she would say about what she offers. Her personality, though, is completely different from mine. Mercedes has a dominant personality. Mine is more submissive, and she read that from me right way. She said, 'Listen, don't let your personality affect the service you provide or what you charge.'"

The rates for a party are up to the woman to set, as an independent contractor, with the exception of parties in the VIP Room with its mirrored ceiling and large bed. There is a minimum rate for the VIP Room.

"I asked Mercedes what she charges for the different parties," Tandy said. "What I found out was that girls were charging anywhere from hundreds to thousands for a standard party. Some charged based on time. Some charged based on the experience."

TANDY'S FIRST PARTY THAT night remains vague in her mind. The doorbell rang — a soft *ding-ding-ding* resonating in both wings of the house — followed by an electronic buzzing that signaled the front door had been opened. A few minutes later, a grating *EHHH* blared in the hallways: a signal activated by the bartender with a button under the bar, summoning the women to assemble in the parlor. The customer had requested a lineup.

The eight working women in the house formed a line in the parlor in advance of walking single-file into the bar room. The general tactic in the house is to stagger the women so no two of the same height or hair color are side by side as they form a row facing the customer. Tandy was the only blonde in his queue. She wound up first in line.

Led by Tandy, the ladies walked into the bar room and spread out in a row. Each, in turn, smiled, said, "Hi" and gave her name to the Latino man facing them. Tandy can't remember much about what he looked like — his face remains a blur — but he was in his early thirties.

He picked her. Her first lineup had yielded her first negotiation.

"I was so nervous," Tandy recalled. "Mercedes, bless her heart, came with me on the tour I gave him of the house, then accompanied us into the Conversation Room. She was just my rock. It was really cool and really weird at the same time, because she's young enough to be my daughter."

Tandy informed the guest of her rate for an hour. He said he only had a third that amount. They agreed to a 20-minute party.

"After I booked his money, he asked if he could finish his drink. I said 'Of course, let me get the room ready for the party.' We have bedsheets we call, 'trick sheets.' Mercedes and I spread a trick sheet over my bed. I grabbed my supplies and then I set the tone for the party. I started the music on my phone: Taylor Swift and love ballads. I turned on my lamps and lit a candle.

"My heart was pounding. I told myself, 'OK, this is twenty minutes of my life. I can do this. And I'm going to be great!'"

She found the young man in the bar and took control of the party then and there. She led him by the hand out the door that led into the old wing, and down the hall to one of the two men's rooms, where she instructed him to take a shower. She waited for him outside.

He emerged freshly cleanse, and she led him through the corridor that led to the new wing, then all the way down the hall to her room at the end.

> Tandy recalled her first party as a courtesan. 'My heart was pounding. I told myself, 'OK, this is twenty minutes of my life. I can do this. And I'm going to be great!'

Inside, she instructed him to undress and stand by the bed. Earlier that day, Mercedes and some other girls had showed Tandy pictures of signs of STIs to look for on male genitalia for the pre-party "dick check." The procedure called for Tandy to pull on a pair of disposable medical gloves then closely inspect the man's private parts for warts, bumps and lesions. She'd also have to peel back the foreskin to check for any discharge — clear, cloudy or bloody — from the urethra.

The young man passed the exam.

"I'm just going to buzz the bar and let them know everything's OK," Tandy told him. That was the system she'd been instructed in, communicating to the bartender via the intercom in her room.

"Thank you, have a good time," the bartender's voice replied.

The party called for straight sex. Tandy undressed, they climbed on the bed, she sat before him on the trick sheet, removed the condom from its packet, positioned it on the head of his penis and slid it on. She eased into the sex. To her relief, it all felt perfectly natural. In fact, it proved to be an a-ha moment: revelation and exhilaration.

Tandy discovered, then and there, that she is, by nature, a warm, sensuous woman who craves kissing, cuddling and nurturing a lover. Even if it's a temporary love: a stranger she'd met only a few minutes before.

Tandy came to learn at Bella's that her instinctual approach to a party actually has a trade term: "the GFE" — standing for "the Girlfriend Experience." Tandy was a natural-born GFE provider.

Her inaugural party progressed seamlessly. It felt good. The young man finished well before the bartender's voice came over the intercom, saying, "Thank you," indicating the allotted time was nearly up and Tandy had to conclude the party.

"I felt so happy that everything went so well — and that he was so happy — that when I walked him back to the bar, I told him he was my very first customer," Tandy said. "I just had to say it."

"You're kidding me!" the man replied.

Tandy left him in the bar and exited into the old wing. Mercedes intercepted her.

"Are you OK?" the big sister asked.

Tandy smiled. "Yeah, I'm perfectly fine."

She was now — officially — a courtesan.

The experience was more than a confidence builder. It was a defining moment for her, Tandy said.

"From then on, I knew I could do this."

TANDY STAYED A MONTH at Bella's that first stint. Even her period didn't keep her off the floor. She used a vaginal contraception sponge. And she continued to enjoy her work. Tandy's sex drive is such that she feels even more sexual during menstruation.

"I get picked like crazy that time of the month," she said. "It may be something to do with the pheromones."

Since starting at Bella's, Tandy didn't take more than two weeks off at a time. She was picked in party after party, establishing herself as one of the most consistently popular women in the house. She got ahead financially. Her great worry about going broke passed.

My guiding influence about setting goals, and projecting oneself for success, took root.

"Her philosophy on the power of positive thinking is all around the house," Tandy said of me. "We're encouraged to write empowerment statements on the whiteboard. At our CB radio station is a calendar, and each day there's a new saying on it. It's in your face here, every day, to be positive and attract good things into your life."

Working as a courtesan has generated self-growth and self-awareness, Tandy said.

"Bella's really encouraged me to be independent, to be comfortable with being on my own. This is the first time in my life I've been out on my own, not surrounded by family, not married. I'm not in my comfort zone. It's been such an enriching experience! I'm living in a house with many different women from all different backgrounds, and we're all here encouraging each other. Not only has it empowered me, but I'm proud that I'm part of empowering other people — the other women in the house. I feel more self-confident, more self-sufficient, than before I came to Bella's."

She also relishes a sense of pride in her newfound profession.

"I make a difference in the lives of the clients who come here. Most of what we do is not sex. These men come in here and they're broken. They have lost their wives, or their best friend, or their girlfriend. Or they are lonely and never really had anyone. They have all these different emotions going on. They long for that touch, that encounter, to feel loved, to feel something. I've been in here with a client who had me in tears, just sharing his story with me, and just feeling like I was making a difference in his life."

Her bedroom has been the setting for tender, rewarding encounters on the queen-size bed with its thick, sage-green chenille spread. The little room is warm and inviting, adorned with stenciled designs and sayings she put on the walls to inspire herself. One wall features large rainbow-colored plastic butterflies and plastic wreaths of white daffodils. On another hangs a rectangular placard painted black, set above a leafy-green plant, bearing these sayings in white block letters: "FOLLOW YOUR HEART"; "BE YOUR TRUE SELF"; "YOU GOTTA DANCE LIKE NOBODY'S WATCHING"; "LOVE AS THOUGH YOUR HEART KNOWS NO BOUNDARIES"; "DREAM LIKE YOU WILL LIVE FOREVER."

Tandy understands her work is vital to society. I moved her to tears one day as we sat in the kitchen, talking about life at the brothel. I sat Tandy down, looked her in the eyes and said, "You are a gift."

"That was just so powerful, the way that she said it," Tandy recalled. "I feel like I'm so much more than a wife and a mother. I have an impact on the world. There's a need for people like us."

TANDY'S SKILLS IN PROVIDING sensual services have increased significantly with experience. She developed her innate talent.

"I'm naturally one to provide the girlfriend experience," she said. "My party is more touch-feely, intimate. It's not robotic. I'm a very sexual person. And most of my parties have been good."

Clients seeking something rough can tell from the discussion in the Conversation Room that Tandy is not the right choice, she said.

"I'm more submissive, I'm not really good at a dom party."

She'll never forget one particular customer who initially wanted to be physically disciplined.

A courtesan bides time, relaxing in her room, between lineup calls. Keeping a positive, playful mindset I critical to her success. *Photo by Victory Tischler-Blue*

"He was in his fifties, a tall, gray-haired man from Portland, Oregon. He was wealthy and retired, and driving around the country in a new RV. The thing I remember most about him was his eyes. *Puppy-dog eyes.* He had hurt in them. He'd lost his wife two years before and was feeling guilty about her passing. He had all these issues."

In the Conversation Room, he explained to Tandy what he had in mind.

"He told me about clubs in Portland you can go to get beaten," Tandy recalled. "He showed me pictures on his phone where he'd been severely beaten. He was doing that as a way of making himself suffer.

"I agreed to do the party, but I told him we were going to do it *my* way. I started the party by playing music and just holding him and slow dancing with him. He's relaxing. I'm giving him this full-on love experience. At the end of it, he just said, 'Thank you. That's the first time I've felt love since my wife passed.'"

Tandy felt elated. It was a tremendous ego stroke to hear she had fulfilled someone's need so profoundly.

"Before coming into this industry, you have this idea that men come in here and they just want sex and that's all they care about," she said. "I've learned it's about *connection*. We're all created to connect, we're all created for each other. A hug is so powerful. Touch is so powerful."

In her down time at the house, Tandy researches sexual techniques by reading articles online or watching YouTube tutorials. Her web research gave her the knowhow to service an obese client whom she found was impossible to have traditional sex with, because his girth interfered. She would have to hold folds of flab apart while reaching his sex organs.

This man, who'd traveled in from Utah, had booked a party with Tandy in the VIP Room. Obviously, the sexual position would be woman on top. It wasn't that simple, though.

"He has circulation issues, because of his physical condition, and he is unable to stay hard very long. I couldn't necessarily ride him into an orgasm. So, I introduced him to a prostate orgasm."

Tandy employed two devices. One was a battery-powered cock-ring with a vibrator.

"I put the ring around his penis and balls, and there's a little vibrator on the bottom of that," she explained. "I'm able to do a hand job. I also have a little dildo I can put a condom on. I penetrate his anus and bring him to a prostate orgasm."

The party was successful. It was a point of pride with her.

Pride in her work — and in herself — leads Tandy to reject clients with bad attitudes.

"They need to have a good attitude. That, to me, is a big deal," Tandy said.

"There are guys who talk down to you because of what you do. You can kind of tell they're almost dismissing you. They're arrogant. Most of the time, I do my best to be really nice about it, then I'll offer to get them another girl.

"There's this group of Russian businessmen who come in, three or four of them. They're in their thirties. I don't know what their profession is. They've been here quite a few times. They are totally pompous. The first two times they came in, the same guy picked me. I'm taking him on a tour, talking to him, sharing about the house and what we offer. I could tell he was not interested. He just wanted to pay and bring me back to the room. I said, 'I don't think we're connecting.'

"Respect goes a long way. No lady needs to be treated like a streetwalker."

SEVEN MONTHS INTO HER career at Bella's, Tandy was proud of working as a "courtesan": the term I insist the women use.

Courtesans — unlike streetwalkers, unlike "prostitutes" — have high professional standards, and, as I continually counsel, set personal goals. They ply their trade as a means to an end: personal empowerment.

Before coming to Bella's, Tandy was floundering in financial straits. Seven months later, she was in the process of buying a house in the Vegas area.

All in all, choosing to work at Bella's proved to be the right move for her. And there was an extra benefit for a woman as sexually primed as she.

"I orgasm like crazy!" she said, laughing her girlish laugh.

* * *

Kayla: Sex therapist with a helping heart

Auburn-haired Kayla is a 36-year-old fireplug of carnality: 5-foot-2 with 40DD breasts, bisexual and into couples. She possesses an encyclopedic knowledge of sex toys and bears a knowing glint in her greenish-blue eyes.

Kayla can provide more than just a mind-blowing party. If you want feedback on your performance, she'll tell you, bluntly, how you did — and explain how to do it better.

In essence, Kayla is a sex therapist. While her personality is strong and assertive — she can take control of the party before the client realizes his wrists are fastened into bed restraints — she has a deeply empathetic streak that drives her to help people become better at sex and in their relationships.

Kayla has a ready sense of humor, with a ready laugh. Yet she takes her sex work seriously. For her, it is more than a way to supplement her and her husband's income.

It's a *calling*.

'Women can earn good money this way, and control their own destiny, and make as much money as they want,' Kayla said. 'And, historically, they've done that.'

"I believe that this business, being the oldest profession out there, we're at the highest form of customer service," Kayla said, as she perched on a black bedspread patterned with red, white and gray flowers in her bedroom. Her short, silky black kimono generously revealed cleavage and milky thighs.

"And we're totally and completely in control," she added. "Women can earn good money this way, and control their own destiny, and make as much money as they want. And, historically, they've done that."

KAYLA THINKS OF HERSELF as a country girl. Her single father, to whom she remains close, raised her on a cattle ranch in northern California outside the town of Yreka. She is of mixed ethnicity, and proud of her Native American lineage in northern California's Karuk tribe.

She already was married with four children when she began in the sex industry.

"My husband got sick and lost his job. He was union. And bills had to be paid."

During this period, they happened to be driving on Interstate 80 in northwest Nevada. They were 20 miles past Reno when they saw a billboard for the Mustang Ranch, which is in Storey County, where brothels are legal.

"I said to my husband, 'Well, I can go be a hooker. I gave it away for free for years. I might as well get paid for it.' You know, just joking."

He took her suggestion seriously.

"We actually spent most of the night looking into it. And the next day, I went and applied. We're still in it together."

Kayla has worked at seven brothels in northern Nevada, with Bella's being the one she prefers. She hasn't concealed her profession from her father.

"My dad knows about every brothel I've worked in. The first time I ever told him, though, he was like, 'Are my grandchildren OK?' I said, 'Yes, they are.' He asked, 'Are you using drugs?' I said, 'No, I'm not.' He said, 'I have nothing to say about it then.'"

As for her children?

"My kids think I'm a server in a motel, because I won't outright lie to them. I refuse to. And that's basically what I *am*. It's an hourly motel, but a motel. I don't want to lie to them about anything."

As for her husband? They have what Kayla called "a very unique relationship."

"When I'm home, I tend to hit up the bars and bring women home with me. My husband and I don't necessarily have an open relationship, but it's open to a certain extent. Most couples in an open relationship are like, 'OK, I'll go see who I want, you go see who you want.' I only do this at work. That's it. When I'm at home, I don't see any other man, ever, other than my husband. We bring women into our relationship because I have an attraction to women, as well. And I see that if I'm at work at a brothel, regardless that I'm getting paid, he should be able to relieve himself, as well."

The brothel career has helped their family because there's no other way Kayla can legally make the same amount of money, she said.

Her husband recovered from his debilitating illness and is working again. He and Kayla are building subcontractors. They remodel homes.

"When business is slow, we'll come back to this," Kayla said.

"Why not? A couple weeks out of the month, it's not bad."

WHAT KAYLA LIKES ABOUT working at Bella's is its rural setting and positive atmosphere.

Ranchers and farmers, hunters and fishermen frequent Bella's. Kayla finds them easy to chat with.

"I'm not a city person, at all. When I get a lot of the city clientele who come in, it just makes me uncomfortable," she said. "I can pretty much talk about anything with anyone — be it political, cultural, educational. But I would prefer to be able to talk to people about what kind of scope they're carrying on their rifle, or what kind of engine they're running under their hood, or the fact I spend more time in steel toes than I do in high heels. It makes me more comfortable that way."

Kayla also appreciates the communal approach I instill among the women in the house.

"A lot of brothels have this thing about favoritism. Some of the brothels are run by previous working girls and they will play favorites, like high school drama style, with girls they have worked with. Bella keeps the drama down here. If there are issues, she addresses them. This house is really comfortable."

As madam, I preach optimism and mutual support among the women. I never tolerate them competing with each other. Kayla says that approach is important.

"When you work with girls who get upset or negative — severely negative — over somebody else booking instead of them, those girls bring everyone down. They bring down the whole aspect of, 'I'm here to work, you're here to work, let's keep it positive.' If I book, I want you to be happy for me, just as I'm happy for you."

Like in many of the bedrooms at the ranch, a wall in Kayla's room bears a stenciled affirmation I affixed: "LIFE is Beautiful," the words laid out between two leafy trees. On another wall is a framed outline of a heart with these words superimposed in black letters: "START EACH DAY WITH A GRATEFUL HEART."

Kayla's personal items give the room an intriguing feel. Among the various garments hanging here and there are a black bra with metal studs, and a pair of pink-and-white bunny ears. Her tools of trade are far more eccentric than the standard basket of foil-packaged condoms to fit various sizes. Among her sex toys:

- The Jack Rabbit: a battery-operated dildo that features a big red rubber shaft and head. A round chamber above the shaft is filled with beads that rotate to provide extra stimulation. On the Jack Rabbit's side is a "clit tickler" with a finger-shaped tip. It is geared to stir extreme arousal.

- A battery-operated double-cock ring. One ring goes around the base of the penis, the other around the testicles. The contraption vibrates and rotates in its center to trigger intense pleasure.

- A mini whip — a black-leather cat o' nine tails — which Kayla favors using on women. "It's soft enough that you can use it. Most people don't realize how erotic it can be to slap the vagina."

- A standard ball gag with holes in it to drain away drool. It serves a second purpose, as well. "I have a lot of clients that don't know how to shut up during sex. They think that most girls want to hear them talk, and we don't! So, I'll put that in their mouth."

- A standard collar with studs. "The great thing about this one, I use this mostly on myself for nuru massages. You use it to massage their body with your body. I wear it to rub all over their neck and back."

- A G-spot finder. "It's hooked and goes up, and you find the shelf where the G-spot is."
- A container of Nipple Nibblers balm: strawberry flavored, and containing numbing menthol.
- A tube of clitoris-sensitizing lubricant. "It helps you come. If you have difficult parties, you slap it on ten minutes before, and you're good to go. It's for when you know things are going to be difficult — or you know that the client is going to continue, and not be able to satisfy himself without knowing that you are satisfied."

Along with her expertise with sex toys and aids, Kayla is astute at intuiting a client's bedroom skills.

"Generally, I can read most people within five minutes of seeing them, talking to them and booking a party, whether they're going to be difficult. Usually, it's the arrogant guys who think they are God's gift to women that are the ones that are difficult. Most of them are so arrogant that they can't relinquish that control, but the minute you get them behind this door, it's totally different. *I* take control. I generally take *severe* control. I'm one of the best!"

She points at the wrist restraints on her bed's headboard.

"Most guys are all for it, because they don't realize what's happening at first. Then they're, 'Oh, wow, I'm going to let you take control, OK.' And they enjoy that.

"This is stuff I do in my everyday life with my husband."

KAYLA IS PARTICULARLY PROUD of servicing clients whose lives she changed for the better.

"I was working for a different brothel, not Bella's. A gentleman came in and none of the other girls would approach him because of how he appeared. Dirty. Grungy. The Sammy Hagar-style hair. Cutoff sleeves. Dirty shoes. They thought he didn't have any money. So, I went up and said, 'Hey, how's it going?'

"I got him to book for an hour. He enjoyed his time so much with me, he came back two days later and booked with me for the entire weekend. And he had the money.

"After partying with me, he gained the confidence to go and speak with the girl that he'd been crushing on for a long time. She was a bartender where he lived in California. He used to go into the bar and talk to her but never stay long. It turned out she had a thing for him, too, but she saw him as insecure. And she was right! But with his confidence up, he got to know her better.

When it comes to BDSM, "Most guys are all for it, because they don't realize what's happening at first. Then they're, 'Oh, wow, I'm going to let you take control, OK.' And they enjoy that,' Kayla said.

"I learned all this because he called me and told me about it, including that they were getting married. It made me feel good! My husband and I were invited to the wedding. We still go over and see them quite often.

"I should explain that there were only a select few clients who had my name and number when I worked at that particular brothel. I'd given them my number because I'd found that some of my high-dollar clients were being re-routed to other girls when the clients emailed that brothel.

"Shortly after the client who I helped get married, I got a call on my cell and another client's name and number popped up. He was a trucker from Nebraska. He'd seen me five or six times. I answered and said, 'Hi sweetheart. What's up?' And it was his *wife!* I didn't know she knew that'd he'd been to the brothel. Well, she did. I was like, 'Uh, how's it going?'

"The first thing out of her mouth was, 'I don't know what you did, I don't know how you did it. But whatever it was, thank you.'

"It turned out he'd slid my phone number up inside the tongue of a tennis shoe, and she'd found it. It had my name and 'Nevada' written on it. Then she went through his bank records of credit-card transactions and noticed he'd used his card at a restaurant in Nevada on a specific day. Then she logged into his computer and went into his location settings in Google Maps and checked out what other businesses were in the vicinity of the restaurant. Even though he'd used cash at the brothel, she figured it out. Women are the best FBI!

"She went to him, and he confessed, because their relationship had become a lot stronger by this time. I hadn't seen him for maybe six months. What he'd learned from me, though, had improved everything in their marriage.

"She said to me, 'I just want to tell you, thank you. What you did saved our marriage. You gave him a point of view that he didn't see before, as to where I was with things. It brought us around.'

"She spent forty-five minutes with me on the phone, explaining how their relationship had gone downhill because he'd become less attentive.

A rear view of courtesans facing a guest in a lineup. *Photo by Laura Higdon*

Basically, it became that she was solely at home to cook and buy groceries and do the laundry and take care of the house, and he was there to say, 'Hi, bye,' and out the door to make another trucking run. She said, 'It basically felt like I was a prostitute. He would come home and give me money to buy whatever I wanted, as long as everything in the house was done. So, I was a married prostitute.'

"The change came after he'd been with me. During those five or six times he'd seen me, I became not only his companion but his therapist. He would talk to me about what was going on at home, and how she was acting. They'd lost their connection. It was gone.

"After our first time together, he'd asked, 'How was it?' I won't lie. If you come right out and ask, I'm going to be brutally honest. I don't sugarcoat anything. And when he asked, I said, 'Well, you know, things could have been better.' And he looked at me like I'd just slapped him in the face. He's like, 'Wait, what?' I'm like, 'Well, you need to take your time more. The penetration aspect is great, you're great at that. But it's leading up to that.'

"He was bad at just being there for someone other than himself. And being married, that isn't good for him! It was get in, get it wet, get out. At home, as well as here. I explained to him that when you walk into the room and see your wife standing at the dresser, or something like that, you *ease into it*. You kiss the back of her neck. You slide your hands down her sides to her hip. You don't go directly for the breasts, the vagina, the ass. You make it sensual. He was just going right for the, 'Hey, bend over, let's do this' type of thing."

Kayla taught him how to be sexually and emotionally intimate.

"After being with me, he felt sexual again. He felt that he could go home and do the things he did with me with her — sexually, conversationally, emotionally. I made him see that his wife could be what I was for him."

Kayla proved to be a marriage saver.

Her frank educational approach can be invaluable.

"Don't ask a question if you don't want an honest answer," she said, "because I will tell you flat out, 'Yeah, you're OK with this'; 'Yeah, you're OK with this'; 'This was great.' I'll walk you through the whole process after the fact, if you'd like. Some people get so offended by the truth. But you'd be surprised at how many people come back and say, 'Wow, I'd like to do *this*, this time.'

"I show them everything from toy play to generally where the G spot is for a woman. It's never in the same place for most women, but you can pretty much find things if you play around a little bit and aren't rushing it.

"My experiences with clients have shown me how them having such a positive outcome in the bedroom can change their lives."

KAYLA BELIEVES BROTHELS SHOULD be legalized across the country.

"There would be less need for pimps, so there would be less violence taken with the girls. And maybe the profession — sex with a random person for money — wouldn't be so looked down on, so taboo."

That, in turn, could have a therapeutic effect throughout society, she said.

Kayla traces the root of mental-health issues that spawn a range of societal woes — from mass shootings to road rage, addiction, depression, and the widespread use of anti-depressants — to a breakdown in the family unit. Instead of parents raising their children, the television, the internet, the cell phone, the nanny does, she said.

A remedy?

"I believe legalizing the sex industry will relieve the aggression in a lot of people. I believe the depression levels for a lot of people will go down, because then they could be happier. Let's say you're sitting at home with your wife and you're in this depressed state, and your wife isn't doing anything for you to help bring you out of that depression. You walk down the street to the nearest brothel, pay a sex worker a certain amount of money, and all of a sudden you're happy, because you have the endorphins running through your system you didn't have before."

However, it's unlikely this widespread legalization will happen in America, she said.

"From a standard, stereotypical woman's perspective, legalizing sex work everywhere is such a negative thing in their mind, because now you don't know if your husband's out there doing it. And people are so stuck on controlling what they have, instead of accepting people for who they are, that now they're forcing them to secretly run into the arms of a sex worker, because they refuse to be open-minded about a few things."

What about Nevada brothels being the model to be used elsewhere in the United States?

Kayla says courtesans can be great sex tutors for clients. 'I show them everything from toy play to generally where the G spot is for a woman. My experiences with clients have shown me how them having such a positive outcome in the bedroom can change their lives.'

"I think they could be," Kayla said. "But then again, you get into the political aspect of it. The women's perspective — from never being in this type of industry — is they look at it as a negative thing. One, they think we sex workers are victimized. They think that this shouldn't be legal. And it leads back into religion. The 'committing adultery' part. The way most women will look at it is, 'If they legalize it throughout the U.S., then how many marriages are really going to last?'"

Kayla noted the irony. There are ample underground businesses peddling sex. Still, the existence of legal brothels around the country would prey on many women's minds, she said.

"They think we take away, or interrupt, or cause issues in their marriage, when in all actuality, we are here to provide a service, and nine out of ten times a husband who comes to us doesn't leave his wife, because he gets what he needs here and goes home. We're not looking to get married to the guy that walks through the door. Yet, what if he goes out to a bar and picks up some girl and gets her pregnant? Guess what, there goes your husband. If he comes here, instead, you have nothing to worry about."

Kayla scoffs at the notion that women working in brothels are victims of society and their circumstances.

"Oh, my goodness, the stereotype from that, 'Oh, I must have had a horrible childhood.' 'Oh, I must have daddy issues.' 'Oh, this . . .'

"I call my dad every day!"

She laughs.

"People don't understand that this is not somewhere you go to work at if you feel insecure or victimized. This is a place you go to feel strong and sure of what you want to do, and who you are. Now, I personally believe that women who do it outside of legal brothels, and that have their pimp controlling their outcome, *are* victimized, because they are being controlled into doing whoever they're told to."

They're typically controlled by violence and drug use, Kayla added.

"Here, you don't have that. I choose who I want to be with, I choose how much I want to charge."

And it's worth the price, she said. The client can be pleasured. The client can be tutored. Afterward, he won't be bothered.

"That's what I tell clients all the time. 'You get the best of both worlds here. You get sex and no drama. We're not calling you the next morning.'"

* * *

Holly: A carnal scholar

Holly is 27, voluptuous, and well-versed in the kinkier options for a sex party. Her mischievous brown eyes and blue- and purple-dyed hair, and her piercings in her septum and philtrum, lower lip and below the chin are clues to her edgy, adventurous nature. She has the look of the dramatic performer and, indeed, relishes indulging in sexcapades: using her bedroom as her stage as she fulfills whatever fantasy role the party calls for.

Holly takes her roles to heart. She views her work satisfying a customer's unique sexual cravings as mental therapy.

Maybe it's engaging in age-play: dressing herself up as an innocent girl in a plaid skirt and meeting up with the neighbor boy next door. Or perhaps it's playing the part of an older woman seducing a young man with her 38DD breasts. Or it could delve into the BDSM realm and involve some combination of chains and ropes, cuffs and collars, gags and gloves, vibrators and cock rings.

Though she's under 30, Holly's versatility is vast. She entered the Bondage, Discipline, Sadism and Masochism community in her native northeast Ohio while in her late teens, fulfilling the role of a submissive. She can switch over to the duties of a dominatrix. She can gushingly ejaculate in a squirting party. And she can wax wonderfully sweet and supportive to provide the GFE (girlfriend experience).

Holly's broad knowledge is a result of her wide-eyed explorations into sexuality that began at age 11, when she asked her mother to buy her a vibrator. Her mother — an independent and liberated woman who encouraged her children to express themselves — obliged.

"I knew about vibrators because I have a sister who is four years older than me, and she read *Cosmo*," Holly explained. "My mom always raised us to be in control of our own sexuality. She was very much about, 'If a man doesn't make you come, you don't fake it. That doesn't do anybody any service.' Every Christmas after she bought me my first vibrator, she got me a new vibrator. When I was 17, she bought me a bottle of Analese, and said, 'Hey, anal will change your life.' Unfortunately, at that age, I didn't know that there's a way of relaxing your muscles. That was just a horrible experience. I've since, thankfully, figured it out: deep breathing, practice meditation. It's worth it. It's very fulfilling.

"Thanks to my mom's openness and acceptance, I learned to embrace my sexuality, and to use this medium to help others express their sexuality safely."

AT 16, HOLLY DECIDED she wanted a career as a burlesque dancer. At 17, her interest switched to porn. She performed in a few amateur videos whose producers wanted to sell to porn sites. "Nothing too big," Holly said. She also did some nude modeling.

At 18, she signed up with an escort service. She had no negative customer experience, yet had to cope with the anxiety of engaging in an illegal enterprise.

What prompted her to consider working for a legal brothel in Nevada was the desire to make good money fast. Married with two young daughters, Holly wanted to earn enough quickly to allow her to be a stay-at-home mom. She searched brothel websites, found the one for Bella's, checked me out online.

For Holly, sex isn't dirty, and sex-for-pay isn't wrong and shouldn't be criminalized and vilified. She perceived me as a pioneering independent woman running her house in a proper fashion.

"I figured if I was going to go anywhere, the house of a woman who's fighting for workers is probably a good bet," Holly explained, sitting in her bedroom, clad in the floral-patterned kimono she'd worn on her honeymoon.

Before traveling from Ohio, she'd also phoned Bella's for more information. Then she'd had a serious chat with her husband.

"I talked with my husband about me getting back into actual

A courtesan peers out a bedroom window, watching for traffic entering the Hacienda's lot. *Photo property of Bella Cummins*

interactive sex work. We hashed it out for a couple months, discussing what were our boundaries, what did we hope to make out of this. Then we decided to do it."

Her husband, Holly said, is the "accepting" type. They have a "semi-open" polygamous relationship that allows each of them to take a female lover. "Men was the one thing off limits. But we talked about what I could make at a brothel, and we set boundaries for what would be specifically for us."

In other words, they reserved certain intimate sexual acts for themselves.

"He was super understanding," Holly said. "And now he's totally cool with it."

Holly cleared several thousand dollars during her initial two-week residency at Bella's. She and her husband were pleased. It meant she didn't need to find another line of work to support their household.

"I'm able to be comfortable and do what I want with my kids and not worry about my bills, while spending quality time at home with them."

HOLLY GREATLY ENJOYS HER work at Bella's. Sensual-service workers are basically educators and therapists, she said. Another humane aspect to the profession is providing a sexual outlet to those who can't find partners elsewhere.

"We get people in here who have physical handicaps, who have mental handicaps, who have emotional handicaps," she said. "Either they can't make that connection with another human being, or people aren't willing to give them the opportunity to make that connection. This is where they can be touched, and learn their comfort level, and get that intimacy. Because every human being needs touch.

"I had one guy for multiple parties. He didn't want to go into full-blown details about what his health problems were, but he had scars straight down his pelvis and pubic bone. And he had incontinence. I serviced him. I made sure he had a shower first. And I wasn't going to make him feel bad about that. He had no control over his health problems."

'We live in a sexually stunted society right now,' Holly says. 'We have this elementary knowledge of what it is to have and express human sexuality. We need people to give a complete sexual education. That's what we do here!'

What special qualities make Holly able to service strangers — including those with disabilities?

"I don't know that it's that you're born able to do something like this," she said. "For me, personally, it's always been that I have a deep compassion for people. And I've always had this complete fascination with sexuality. It was crazy to me that my friends couldn't ask their parents questions about sex. So, they asked me."

The role of sexual educator is a noble and necessary occupation in America, Holly said, and she's passionate about it. The parties she performs with patrons at Bella's can provide more than mind-blowing pleasure and wild thrills, she explained.

They can be liberating.

"We live in a sexually stunted society right now. We have this elementary knowledge of what it is to have and express human sexuality.

At this point in our country, we can't even agree on the definition of consent. We need people to give a complete sexual education. That's what we do here! You may not know how to pleasure a woman, but you can come in here and learn, because we're not going to just lie to you. If you want to know the truth, OK, we'll tell you.

"We'll also teach you how to protect yourself, because we use condoms, and we use a dental dam or a female condom for performing cunnilingus, so you don't get any fluids in your mouth. It will protect you from contracting a sexually transmitted disease or infection from giving a woman oral sex. People don't think about oral transmission. A lot of customers, when they come here, learn the importance of condoms, because you're not getting anything without a condom on your penis, and you're not allowed to give me oral without protection. It registers in their mind, 'What, you can get something from this?'

"We have a very elementary-level education in our schools when it comes to sex and sexual expression. A brothel can be an important educational resource. Instead of these young boys in their age 18 and 19 college years going out and screwing everybody and spreading things — or being irresponsible, maybe not fully understanding consent — they could instead come here or another local brothel and have those conversations with a woman who has experience. In this environment, there is openness. We are professionals. When there is an exchange of money, there is a dropping of their walls. It's like seeing a therapist. You're paying me to care. So, I'm not going to judge you. It's a safe place to share whatever insecurities they have or have learned, and to move forward."

Moving forward to sexual health involves coming to a point of self-acceptance, Holly said. She sees a lot of anger in America stemming from sexual frustration rooted in ignorance.

"We're in a society where we feel uncomfortable saying to our partner, 'Hey, I like to be slapped a little bit.' Or, 'Hey, y'know, as a man, I like to dress up as a woman sexually. It gets my rocks off.' We're in this society where it's like, 'Oh, no. Bad.' However, it's not! If you're an adult, and they're an adult, do whatever you want as long as it's safe, sane and consensual. It's not hurting anyone."

AMERICAN SOCIETY WOULD BENEFIT immensely from the legalization of brothels, which would even combat the spread of sex trafficking, Holly said.

"In Ohio, they decriminalized sex work for the workers, and then made the sentencing a lot stricter for the johns. So, it's terrifying for the men right now. They're having 15 men arrested in one night. Teachers. Lawyers. Police catch a lot of customers in their net. This is destroying men's lives, and their families, because they are charged with sex trafficking instead of solicitation."

The thrust of the Ohio policing is to combat sex trafficking, but it won't work, Holly said. What would work, she said, is legalizing sex-for-hire the way Nevada has, by allowing counties to decide when and where to permit legal brothels.

"If Ohio's state legislators gave us legal status, it would limit the amount of profit sex traffickers could make, while offering the trafficked women the opportunity to get out through the network of sisterhood found in brothels.

"I personally think that Nevada is one of the only constitutional states left, and the state should be proud of that. I believe more states need to adopt this approach. Do I think it will ever happen? I hope that it will."

The language in Nevada statutes permitting brothels needs updating, Holly said.

"There needs to be differentiation between us — the legal, licensed workers — and illegal 'prostitutes.' I feel like if a woman is doing this legally, she shouldn't be labeled the same thing as someone who can be charged with doing it illegally. I don't care if they call us 'legal sex workers' or 'courtesans' or 'intimate service providers,' but make that distinction. That word, 'prostitution,' implies nasty and distasteful, and I'm not doing nasty and distasteful work.

"People misunderstand, thinking that this work is somehow sad. It isn't. I personally have social anxiety, so I benefit from my interaction with each client. And we courtesans are really helpful to our clients. They leave happy. They leave with more confidence. They're able to go out into the world and be in non-transactional relationships, because they get confidence from their experience at Bella's. This gives clients an opportunity to learn social skills without shame or feeling less than adequate. They've grown as lovers and in sexuality. They also realize they can talk to a woman. We love to talk. We talk a lot!"

She laughed.

"I'm one of them. I never shut up!"

* * *

Lisa: A free-spirited Asian beauty

When Lisa is at Bella's, she's sometimes the only Asian woman in the house — which gives her an exotic allure. Tall and slender, dusky and deep-voiced, Lisa is obviously foreign-born with her thick Korean accent.

Two factors ultimately attracted her to the sex industry: the chance to make good money; the opportunity to have lots of sex.

Lisa enjoys sex — a *lot*.

After coming to America as a young woman, she found that her deficient literacy in English limited her job opportunities. She worked in restaurants: waiting tables, cocktail waitressing and bartending. She discovered that moonlighting for an escort service maximized her earning power. A free-spirited, independent soul, she resolved to live her life to the fullest, traveling and experiencing the world, instead of spending her precious years on Earth grinding out a survival income.

Lisa's first experience in the sex industry was with an escort service in a major East Coast city. She answered calls from clients staying in hotels

A cowboy cools his heels at the bar, in the company of a courtesan. *Photo by Victory Tischler-Blue*

or apartment buildings. There were a few nasty encounters, including with a man who held a knife to her throat.

Lisa invested her earnings in property when the housing market was exploding. After the market crashed in 2008, it wiped out her investments.

She had never worked for a legal brothel before contacting Bella's Hacienda Ranch. She pulled her first stint at Bella's in 2011, as the economic recovery remained slow. After a second stay in 2014, she didn't return until Thanksgiving Day 2018. This time, she worked at the ranch through New Year's Day. She returned again in June 2019.

Two reasons explain why she favors working at Bella's. The first is as simple as it gets:

"We make money. That's the most important thing."

The second reason is that I — as madam — foster an optimistic atmosphere for the working ladies, inspiring them to support each other, and to project themselves for success by focusing their minds on attracting customers and making good money. In other words: setting goals and manifesting them through the power of positive thinking.

"It's hard for me to explain in English what Miss Bella has taught me," Lisa said, as she reclined in a black negligee on her room's bed, which was covered with a spread in a black-and-white zebra pattern. "I've never seen anyone like Miss Bella who has so much focus and ideas that she does. I admire her. That's one of the reasons I come here, because of Miss Bella. She has taught me to be strong inside. She is such a positive person. I'm still learning to be more positive."

Not getting picked from a line-up can be a blow to a woman's self-esteem, and the stress can accumulate with repeated rejections. While Lisa is prone to battle through her blues by herself, she appreciates the pep talks I give the women. She said the positive climate I nurture at Bella's — including posting positive affirmations on the whiteboard in the kitchen — is necessary to boost their moods, which can swing up or down depending on how much they're earning.

While there are men who come to Bella's and are compelled by Lisa's looks, others pass her over because of her race.

Rejection stings.

"Everybody's different. That's what is unique about homo sapiens," Lisa said. "My nose looks like a truck ran over it; a Caucasian nose is higher up. We are different, but we are the same people."

The customers who tend to pick her are older white men who are single or unsatisfied in their relationships. "They have no wife, or maybe the wife died, or they got divorced, or they want to kick their girlfriend out, and want to make sure they have somebody," Lisa said.

Then there are those prompted by curiosity.

"Maybe they want an Asian girlfriend or something. When I was working in another area, in a big city, I didn't have that kind of reaction. Here at Bella's, a lot of the guys come from Idaho, Wyoming or Utah, where there are not that many Asians around. They look at me and say, 'You're the first Korean I've ever been with.'"

On the downside, these men can harbor misconceptions about Asian women, believing they are submissive and will automatically give the man royal treatment, like a Geisha girl would. The reality is that Asian women are no more subservient than women of other races or ethnicities, Lisa emphasized.

"I speak my mind."

While that may surprise some customers, Lisa said, they always leave her parties happy.

ONE THING SEX WORKERS learn in a brothel is that customers often are craving attention and affection even more than sex. Lisa learned that, yet maintains that the sex, itself, is vital to their temperament.

"I think without the sex; they will still be grumpy."

She does take pains with those who are feeling low to put them in a better mood by offering perspective.

"I tell them everything will be OK, that they're just like one of us. Everybody, we are all the same people. I tell them that somedays are happy, somedays not, get over it. Sometimes, that changes their mood."

The attitude-elevating ability of sex workers proves their value to society, Lisa said.

"A man, for some reason, if they don't get sex for a long time, or attention for a long time, from either their wife or girlfriend, or they don't have anybody, they are pretty much very, very tense. Most men who come here — it doesn't matter how grouchy they were outside — they come here, they're naked, we're naked, they're always happy! I'm very lucky that men are very nice to women when it comes to the sex part. They come here, if their face doesn't look happy, if they look grumpy, when they leave here, they really have a smile on their face."

Her ability to quickly brighten a person's day — "instant happiness," as Lisa puts it — is extremely gratifying to her. It's a nice dividend of her work.

"If someone's happy, I'm happy," she said, succinctly.

A legal brothel is a safety valve for society, Lisa stressed. Without access to a legal, regulated brothel, a sex seeker would be taking a potentially large risk.

"They're looking for opportunities to have sex anywhere, everywhere," Lisa said. "These days, they have the Internet, and the guys usually tell me they go online and there are all kinds dating sites. That probably didn't work for them, so they are looking for somewhere else to go."

Without a chance to release their sexual tension, to enjoy companionship, Lisa said, "They would be pretty upset. In my mind, they could get violent or dangerous."

Lisa learned the hard way how dangerous working in the sex industry outside of a brothel can be.

While engaged with an escort service in an East Coast metropolis, she reflexively avoided responding to calls that would take her to a bad part of town. There was one call, though, she took at an apartment building that was in what she called a "borderline" area.

"The guy pulled a knife when I asked for money. He held the knife at my throat and said, 'Be quiet.' He wanted to rape me. I said to him, 'The escort service knows where I am at, and if anything happens to me, the mafia will come and either kill you or make you regret what you did.'

"We were wrestling, I'm struggling to get out. I finally got out."

She joined a different escort service. However, she could never get over her reflexive fright every time she arrived at a client's address.

"Before I knock on the door, I always get a nervous breakdown."

Bella's has turned out to be an easier environment to work in than taking illicit outcalls.

"It is so much more relaxed, and the clientele are mostly not really old and grumpy. They're really nice. And it's really, really safe here."

LISA DOES MISS THE good money she made in her youthful past.

"Now, I'm kind of picking up the breadcrumbs, compared to what I used to make."

Still, the money's decent. Working in the sex industry has allowed her to live her life on her own terms. Traveling is one of her passions. Clients she met as an escort have taken her on extensive trips. She's toured in Europe, Asia and Africa.

"Sometimes, it's very exciting," Lisa said. "I've enjoyed many good voyages. I travel a lot, and my goal is I would like to travel some more. Before, all the materialistic things were important for me — having a house, investing. I lost all my money when the real-estate market crashed. Maybe I extended too much. Whatever money that I have, though, I'm not going to take it with me, so I like to travel."

Working in the sex industry has afforded Lisa one of life's most cherished luxuries: free time to enjoy herself.

> 'This industry is like instant love,' Lisa says. 'Everybody throws money — a few hundred or thousand dollars — to make themselves happy. On top of that, if you like the guy — you have some type of physical connection or attraction — that makes it really better. I like almost every single customer. Just a few customers I like way more than others.'

"Time is extremely valuable in a person's life," she said. "God gave us only one hundred years, maximum, so I want to enjoy my life."

In addition to traveling, Lisa enjoys cooking, and has scribbled down hundreds of recipes from cooking classes or YouTube tutorials — although the tutorials are difficult for her to follow, given that she is not a native speaker of English.

"My English is handicapped, and I don't have many opportunities to work in a regular job that makes good money. But working a regular job, whatever I did, I'd just pay the rent and never save any money. This job is reasonable money, plus you get sex. Everybody loves sex.

"This industry is like instant love. Everybody throws money — a few hundred or thousand dollars — to make themselves happy. On top of that, if you like the guy — you have some type of physical connection or attraction — that makes it really better. I like almost every single customer. Just a few customers I like way more than others. It's not even if it's a younger guy or older guy. Some men and women just have more physical chemistry."

Lisa definitely believes brothels should be legal everywhere: "The world would be happier, less grumpy. A safer place!"

But she strongly doubts brothels will be legal in the United States, outside of Nevada, any time soon.

"This country is Christian and very conservative. It probably is not going to happen for another few thousand years."

* * *

Rosie: Selling a service with a smile

Rosie looks like a Caribbean delight. She has a mocha complexion, thanks to her Afro-Cuban heritage. She has a thick, shapely build: 36DD breasts and a great ass. At 26, her skin is smooth, her face is model pretty. Her teeth are straight and white, as befits a trained dental assistant. And she enjoys the greater flow of income she earns at Bella's, compared to her prior career cleaning teeth and assisting with filling cavities.

Providing a different kind of oral care (among other sensual services) pays a lot better.

Rosie is bisexual and enjoys couples. Sex work has been a good fit for her. What led her into it was economic reality.

A FIRST-GENERATION Cuban-American, Rosie grew up in Florida. After high school, she earned an associate's degree in dental assisting. She moved cross country to San Francisco in 2017 to take a job in a dental office. Her compensation was $22 an hour plus full health benefit. It wasn't enough to survive on in one of the most expensive cities in America. The monthly rent on her studio apartment was $2,600. Rosie needed supplemental income. Moonlighting selling sex looked like the way to get good cash fast.

Rosie quickly found she could make more in an hour on a date booked through an escort service than she could in two workdays at the office.

"I used an online escorting site," Rosie explained as she sat in her room, wearing a geisha robe over a black one-piece negligee.

"You post an ad, post pictures. Someone will message you. I had a texting app on my phone, so I didn't have to give out my real number. We'd communicate that way and meet up at a hotel."

Rosie did her best to vet a contacting client on the phone, and if she agreed to meet up at a hotel, they'd proceed first to some public area — maybe a bar — so she could further scope him out and decide if he was dangerous. She also asked for payment first. If the client wasn't willing to pay up front, she'd terminate the date.

Even these precautions didn't allay the worry she always felt going to meet a client. "I had horrible anxiety all the time," she said.

The typical customer was a businessman or professional in his forties or fifties. These men could afford to pay well.

As a rule, her dates went well. One, however, ended badly. It was 18 months into her escort career, as Rosie recalled:

"He said, 'I'll pay you half first, half later.' He felt like I would probably rob him or something. So, I agreed. At the end, I asked for the rest of the money. He didn't really want to pay. We went back and forth. Then he grabbed me by the throat."

He wasn't large, maybe 5-foot-9 and with an average build. Yet he was intent on manhandling her.

"I backed off. I didn't want to get hurt," Rosie said.

This experience is what drove her to consider working in a legal brothel. She hadn't even known such places existed in next-door Nevada until she happened to catch a news story about them on the *VICE* cable-television network.

"That caught my interest," Rosie said. "I just started doing research online."

The larger houses she checked out on websites "seemed a little overwhelming, just because of thirty girls in a house together," she said. Also, she didn't want to end up in a spotlight. The Moonlite BunnyRanch — the best-known Nevada brothel, in Mound House east of Carson City — seemed too high-profile for her. She discovered that the ranch and its late owner, Dennis Hof, had been featured in numerous TV and radio shows and magazine and newspaper articles over the years, including *HBO's Cathouse: The Series*, and *The Howard Stern Show*.

"I read about Dennis Hof and watched interviews and specials about him, and that really kind of turned me off about it," Rosie said. "I didn't want too much publicity. I wanted anonymity."

Rosie called a few other houses. When she phoned Bella's, she spoke with the manager-bartender, who was upfront in answering Rosie's questions. What further persuaded Rosie to venture the 600 miles from San Francisco to Wells was Googling my name and finding the *Wall Street Journal* article from 2002 that reported on a spike in brothel business from the Winter Olympics being held that year in Salt Lake City. The *Journal* reporter had visited the ranch and interviewed me. My quotes published in the article made me sound like a respectable, responsible business owner. That appealed to Rosie. So did my gender.

"I felt like she'd be a little more understanding about our needs and feelings about being in the sex industry," Rosie said of me.

IN MARCH 2019, ROSIE quit her job at the dental office, vacated her San Francisco apartment, packed up and moved out to the ranch with a few belongings. She drove the nine hours on Interstate 80 to Wells battling nerves. Once past Sparks, Nevada, and out in the hundreds of miles of rugged brown hills, playas and sagebrush prairies, she relaxed in the stark peaceful beauty of the Silver State.

Working in a brothel has developed her mental discipline, Rosie said. The moment a party is over with a challenging client and he has been ushered back to the bar, he's out of sight, out of mind. Rosie's night continues: waiting for the buzzer to signal another lineup.

Rosie's worries returned after she arrived at Bella's. Her previous experience selling sex was through the escort service, booking parties from clients who'd read her profile online. Now she would have to sell herself in person, face to face.

"I was terrified," Rosie said.

I paired her up with a "big sister" mentor: Tandy, the most popular choice in lineups. Little blond Tandy is 38 (though could pass for 15 years younger), kind-hearted and, with a teenage son, emotionally mature. She could simultaneously calm Rosie's qualms and mentor her in the little tricks of the trade.

To prep her for her first night on the floor, Tandy brought Rosie into the bar and explained about the lineup and the Conversation Room. It's common for the big sister to accompany the little sister into the Conversation Room when the little sister is booking her first party. Tandy, however, was busy with her own party when Rosie was picked out of the lineup by a fiftysomething trucker.

She was fortunate: The man was considerate. The 30-minute party didn't end up including sex.

"He just wanted to cuddle and play with my boobs," Rosie said. "My first party was an easy one."

From there, she got into the flow of business. The customers generally weren't as affluent as the doctors, lawyers and professionals in the high-tech or financial industries she'd serviced in San Francisco, but she still earned a nice stack of cash by the end of her first three weeks. She also found she much preferred working at the ranch to plying her trade with the escort service — always worried about encountering a sketchy or violent client, or a police detective.

Rosie settled into Bella's to stay indefinitely. The one week a month she doesn't work because of her menstrual cycle, she drives back to San Francisco to see friends. She also takes time off when she likes. She planned a month-long summertime visit to her family in Florida. As an independent contractor, she can plot out her own schedule.

Rooming at Bella's allows her to save a great deal on living expenses. There is no more San Francisco housing-market hemorrhaging. And she doesn't miss being a dental assistant.

IT'S NOT ALL CUDDLES and easy cash, however, at the ranch. Some parties are not too appealing for Rosie.

"The worst parties are the really heavy truckers," she said.

She manages to get through them and provide good service by flipping a switch in her mind.

"I just put on a show, not really think about it too much," Rosie said. "I always start out with a massage or something, and spend as much time as possible away from the sex," she said with a laugh. "Just get them comfortable, give them a massage, and talk. Take my time."

Should a client reek of body odor, she'll have him shower before the party. Occasionally, even a shower doesn't prevent a client from stinking from perspiration during the party. Rosie grins and bears it, as she does with clients with unsightly teeth (which repel her, given her previous career).

Working in a brothel has developed her mental discipline, Rosie said. The moment a party is over with a challenging client and he has been ushered back to the bar, he's out of sight, out of mind. Rosie's night continues: waiting for the buzzer to signal another lineup.

Some specific parties do stick in her memory. The worst request she's fielded was from a client who booked a straight-sex party, then asked for something weird after they were in her room.

"He wanted to sniff my butt. I told him, 'You gotta tip me more.'"

He agreed. Throughout the party, Rosie prayed he wouldn't ask her to fart on him.

The best parties?

"If they're more attractive, maybe younger guys my age, guys who kind of groom themselves a little better. Or fast parties. They'll book an hour and come in like two minutes. The rest of the time is talking. Or sometimes they just say, 'OK, I'll go.' They don't care to hang out."

Rosie learned a great deal her first three months at Bella's. One lesson was how to effectively sell herself to a client, to ensure a party is booked.

"Bella said, 'Always smile.' That works. Being at the front of the line always helps, too, because often the guy picks the first girl that he sees. After you're picked, you just be seductive, touch them, make eye contact, put your hand on their leg, take them on the tour, ask them about their personal lives, 'Where're you coming from?' Once you get them in the Conversation Room, you want to sit really close to them, look into their eyes, say, 'Oh, what kind of party you looking for?' I never sell time. I always sell the actual experience. And that's what gets it sold."

It's an excellent sales tactic: Paint a rosy fantasy in the prospect's mind, then close the deal by offering the terms of fulfilling that fantasy.

ROSIE INTENDS TO WORK in the brothel business until age 32, when she believes she'll have reached her financial goals.

"I want to get a house. That's goal number one. I want to live in

Florida, maybe Sarasota. I just want to save as much as I can."

She's learned some life lessons from me about how an independent woman can get ahead in life.

"To embrace yourself and be confident, and always be positive," Rosie said. "Your energy is everything. The energy you put out is very important."

She understands the value she brings to a customer's life. And she appreciates the value a brothel brings to sex workers such as herself.

Courtesans are masters of small talk. Here a lady shares a drink with a patron at the Hacienda bar. *Photo by Brandi Betancourt*

Rosie's thoughts on brothels becoming legal elsewhere in the country?

"Can it happen? I'm not sure, because there's such a stigma. And not many people know about the brothels in Nevada."

If the Silver State model spread elsewhere in the country, she opined, the brothels would have to be located away from schools and residential areas, as they are in Nevada: situated in discreet locations well out of the public eye. After all, a prime appeal to customers and sex workers, alike, is preserving the privacy of their business, she said.

Legal brothels wouldn't work in jam-packed San Francisco, Rosie said. However, they could work in outlying counties such as Marin or Napa. The residential populations in those counties are affluent — which could add up to lucrative houses, she noted.

"They would make hella money."

* * *

Lacey: A fantasy fulfiller, Marriage saver

Hour-glass Lacey— 38-30-36 — is gifted at helping clients who come to her with personal fantasies to live out. She turns those make-believe scenarios into lasting memories.

It's the same with a client's specific sexual quirks. As Lacey says in her profile on Bella's Hacienda's website: "Come to me with any fetishes or role play. I am a willing partner."

The petite (5-foot-3), busty brunette is equally proud of her open-mindedness and her mindful attention to satisfying a customer's erotic eccentricities and unrequited desires. And if a man, woman or couple wants to play pretend, Lacey is game.

If it's bondage or discipline the client is after, she will oblige that, too. Lacey can take on the dominant or submissive role.

Sexual gratification comes in varieties limited only by human imagination and formative experiences, and therefore is practically infinite in its variety. Lacey — a self-described "mistress of the sheets" — has accumulated a vivid mental archive of parties since beginning her career in sensual services in 2011, when she first came to Bella's.

She was in her early thirties then, a twice-divorced single mother with two sons, and had never worked in the sex industry.

"I did this on a whim," Lacey recalled, speaking with the trace of a warbly twang remaining from her Southern upbringing. "I was in my early thirties, fresh out of a long-term relationship. I just decided I was going to come do it."

She found the environment at Bella's to her liking.

"Every time I came here, I felt comfortable. I felt I was learning more, and growing more as a person. It gave me something to look forward to as I would schedule myself to come back. It's just comfortable here. It's really Bella who has kept bringing me back."

Lacey continued working off and on at Bella's for the next eight years. Just after New Year's Day 2017, she showed up at the ranch after a year's absence. A lot had transpired with her in that period. She arrived with a man she was planning on marrying. She was several months pregnant. He was sickly. They were penniless. They'd run into some hard luck.

I helped them get back on their feet. I hired Lacey as a daytime bartender and put her fiancé to work as a waiter at Bella's Restaurant & Espresso, in Wells. Lacey delivered a healthy baby boy and the family of three moved to Indiana, where the man had relatives. Yet misfortune continued dogging them. Sadly, he passed away not long after from his ailments. Lacey moved to Florida, where her sister lived and could watch after her infant son.

As Lacey worked her way through grief, she returned to Bella's to begin getting ahead financially.

As before her hiatus, she discovered this work to be rewarding.

Now she's thinking about taking over ownership of the ranch someday, after I retire. She sees sensual services as her calling.

"I ENJOY WHAT I do, and I think I've affected a lot of people's lives," Lacey explained. "I'm even surprised at how many people's lives I've affected. I've had a few come back to me and tell me that. Men who've lost their wives. Men who can't find a girlfriend. There've even been some virgins. That's a really neat experience for me! They want their first time to be special."

Lacey recalled two of these deflowering sessions.

"Four years ago, I had a gentleman come in. He'd traveled from out of state. He was twenty-two or twenty-three, a little heavier-set white gentleman. A very nerdy guy. He came in with a laptop under his arm. He was also carrying a little bag. We thought maybe he wanted to take a shower or something. The laptop, it turned out, was to play his music.

He had a whole playlist prepared. It was soft music, nothing aggressive, no rap.

"As I sit him down and start to talk to him about what he liked, he explains straight up that he's a virgin. He pulls out this sheet of paper from the little bag and says, 'These are the things that I want to do and experience.'

"What's crazy is — honestly — if he hadn't told me he was a virgin or spoken about all the things he wanted to do, I wouldn't have guessed. He did them very well! He had a specific list of different ways and different positions. Never just missionary position or doggy style. He had me go on my side and lift my leg up. We did reverse cowgirl. He obviously watched a lot of porn.

"The really strange thing was how the party ended. I thought it was going to last a lot longer. He got to the point where he was about to finish, and asked me if he could do it by himself. Of course, I said yes. He pulled out and took off the condom and he finished. Maybe it's because he'd been playing with himself for so long, that's what he was used to. Or maybe it felt more special to him that way, for his first time. I really have no idea.

"Another virgin I partied with was a Hispanic guy in his thirties. He had gone to prison as a virgin, had been in for a long time, had a lot of tats. He got out of prison and came here to have sex, because he'd never had sex. He was so nervous!

"It was a pretty easy party. Unlike the nerdy young guy, this guy apparently didn't watch porn. He questioned why I didn't have hair down here. I smiled."

SERVICING A COUPLE WITH marital woes is completely different from providing inaugural intercourse with a virgin. Yet the post-coital gratitude is equally profound, Lacey said.

"There've been a few couples I've had over the years where the woman comes back to me later and thanks me for saving their marriage. It had been to that point.

"One of those couples sends me a gift once a year to remind me they're still out there and they still appreciate what I did for them. The wife had me fuck her husband in front of her. It just solved every problem in their marriage. It allowed her to see that the sex was just a physical act. They couldn't have gotten that in traditional marriage counseling."

The reason the wife wanted to see her husband having sex with another woman is that she'd discovered he'd visited Bella's on his own.

"She was really heated," Lacey said. "They were going to get divorced. However, before they got divorced, she wanted to figure out why he liked it so much, so she came here with him, to witness it with her own eyes.

"The woman, actually, is a well-known poet. I can't reveal who she is, but I can say she's published a lot of books. We girls in the house, though, didn't know that about her, or know that her husband had been here before, or that she'd shown up with him out of angry curiosity. Every once in a while, a couple comes in. So, here was another couple. They looked to be in their late forties or early fifties.

"We do a lineup, and she lets her husband pick the woman. He picks a little smaller blonde. The girl gives them a tour of the house. There doesn't turn out to be a party, though. What happened was, the tour made the wife a little bit upset because the girl paid all her attention to the husband and didn't really speak to the wife.

"Bella came to me and asked if I would give them 'the right kind of tour' and find out what's really going on. I said, 'Of course.' When it comes to those kinds of situations when a man and a woman come in, I'm going to talk to the woman. She's the one who's going to make the rules. So, I gave them the tour, and that's when she let me know exactly what was going on. She said she just wanted to see this happen — to see her husband with one of the working girls — so she could know it was just a physical act, and that there weren't actual feelings like she had with her husband.

"So, we did our party. She sat in the chair right there next to us. She didn't say a word. I'm on the bed. She bragged about his dick. It was very curved. It really hooked around. She swore she'd broken his dick.

> Servicing a couple with marital woes is completely different from providing inaugural intercourse to a virgin. Yet the gratitude is equally profound, Lacey says. One couple sends her a gift once a year to remind her they still appreciate she did for them. They couldn't have gotten that in traditional marriage counseling.

"We did our thing. We just had sex. I was on top. It didn't even last that long. We got done, and afterward she gave me a hug. Then she interviewed me, as well as some of the other girls. I'm actually in one of her books. There's an actual story about this, about what happened, mixed up among the poems. They're real raw, raunchy poems. She sent me an autographed copy of the book.

"Anyway, the party saved the marriage. She didn't divorce her husband. Her opinion about him going alone to the brothel had changed.

"Maybe she was using me for her art. If that helped her learn more about what we do and what we're here for, that's fine. Her poetry spreads the word, as well, so why not?

"To this day, five or six years later, she and her husband send me a gift once a year: lots of lingerie, or really pretty outfits. They send a card with the gift. It makes me smile, knowing that I did that for them. It's definitely satisfying, gratifying. I feel really good about it."

THE RANGE OF CLIENT requests never ends for Lacey.

"You get gentlemen who come in with fantasies, things they can't have fulfilled in their regular life. I had an anesthesiologist come in one time. When he was eleven, he got his first hard-on. It was from watching an actress on TV lying on a gurney. It was Shannon Tweed, on the soap opera *Days of Our Lives*. She was passed out, and it really turned him on.

"To this day, he lives with his fantasy of seeing women knocked out on a gurney. He came here to role-play that with me. He had me lie down and he put a surgical cap over my hair. It all had to be tucked in. Then he had me pretend I was going under. He didn't even have intercourse with me. All he wanted to do was touch every part of me. Then he had me come out of the fake anesthesia. And then he slow danced with me, to an Eighties ballad.

"He was so happy when he left. I guess he'd attempted the experience two other times, and whoever the ladies were hadn't understood where he was coming from. It was a really neat experience — even for me."

Another customer's fantasy was of the girl-next-door variety. *Literally.*

"Just recently, I had a gentleman come in and he had a complete descriptive list written all out, to let me know what he wanted me to do. When he was about twelve years old, he would peek on his neighbor as she got undressed. He would spy on her every day. She was a little bit older than him. From his house, he could see into her room. He watched her one time in the bathtub. He swears she did it on purpose.

"His directions were that he wanted me to be in the bathtub as he came into the room, and catch me in the bathtub. I had to completely act this role: "Oh, my gosh!"

"Then I had to tell him, 'You are such a bad boy!' and then say, 'Well, let me show you what a bad boy does' — and make him fuck me.

"It was a pretty interesting role play he had going there."

Lacey knows that many of her parties are profoundly therapeutic.

"I have a client who used to be a police officer. His whole therapy is from me flogging him, and him being blindfolded and hearing stories of me being with other people. He said that being a police officer — on that authority level — for so long, it's therapeutic for him to have to be submissive to someone. It puts him in a whole other place in his mind where he can have peace."

Lacey has to put herself into a different place in her mind from her natural state in order to play the role the ex-cop requires.

"In truth, I'm kind of a submissive person," she said. "However, here at Bella's, I can be the dominatrix. I have the flogger, the paddles, the corsets and the fishnets."

It's part of her job. And she never knows what she might be asked to do to provide sexual therapy.

"The therapy comes in all different ways," Lacey said. "I used to have a gentleman who wanted me to pee in a cup, and just pay me for my pee so he could drink it. I don't judge anyone for anything they come to me with. I do have my limits to what I will do. I will turn down anything to do with number two.

"I understand, though. Everyone has their own thing."

THE FUTURE FOR LACEY?

"I look up to Bella. If I could be in her shoes one day, there's not another woman that I'd want more to be like. She's had a big impact on my life in so many ways — everything from going through a pregnancy in my late thirties, to going through someone passing away I was about to get married to. She has just been there for me through everything, and she's always supported me and always had such great advice for me. I don't know what it is about her, but she is amazing, just as a person.

"Bella has instilled faith in me that I can reach my dreams. She's taught me just to believe in it, and know that it's coming for you, and whatever you want out there will come to you, as long as you believe that it will, and you take action to make it happen. The Law of Attraction works. It's just the positivity you put out in the universe."

Lacey has watched how my campaign to instill optimism in the working women at the ranch — counseling them to write down their goals, then envision those goals coming to fruition — has influenced the type of women working at the ranch.

"It's attracted much better girls who want to be here — girls who are just happy — and it's attracted customers," Lacey said. "Sometimes, we'll do a little money chant. If things are a little slow, we all gather in a circle in the kitchen, hold hands and chant for the money. As we come together, you can just feel the energy building, like a tornado. And I swear, right after that, business gets going.

'Sex is a human need.' Lacey says. 'It doesn't even have to be intercourse. Sexuality has to do with so many other things. Legally, in most places besides here, you're not allowed to explore those things unless you have someone who agrees with you to do it.'

"Bella has taught us about female empowerment. It's knowing we have the ability and the choice to do exactly what we want to do and manifest what we desire in our lives. Being empowered is us knowing that, and using whatever ability we have to get where we need to in life, and becoming more of who we came to be in the second decade of a feminine millennium."

What's the future for the brothel industry?

My own grand plan is to change the attitude in American society toward the brothel industry, so that it will become legalized nationwide. Another aim is to make the word "prostitution" fall from usage, replaced by "sensual services."

Lacey is fully in support of this campaign.

"We ladies are, in a way, sex therapists, as I've been saying. I don't look at us in the way that we are commonly portrayed. Sex is a human need. It doesn't even have to be intercourse. Sexuality has to do with so many other things. Legally, in most places besides here, you're not allowed to explore those things unless you have someone who agrees with

Serena, a veteran courtesan, gazes out at the parking lot as she takes her shift on the CB radio. *Photo by Honey Bee*

you to do it. You can't just pay someone. If it could just be understood that that release — that sexual need that everyone has — deserves to be serviced, and that if there were somewhere people could go to legally fulfill that, it would help them, and help them be a better person.

"If it were legal, for so many people without other options it would help with their anxiety, their stress. I can't even explain all the ways it would help these people if they just had the opportunity to release these desires, which they can't do now unless they do it illegally. And if they do it illegally, it creates even more stress for them. They could get hurt, robbed, arrested, lose their job. They could contract a disease. Syphilis is the number one STD running around right now. It's terrible!

"If this were legal, that wouldn't be the case. In Nevada, we have regulations for brothels. We're tested weekly. Everything is protected. This should be legal in every state. It would help so much in preventing the spread of disease and preventing sex trafficking. It would be the solution for it, if they would just make it legal across the United States.

"The time has come for mankind to be human correctly."

CHAPTER SIX

Madam Bella Raises the Bar

The five-hour drive from my ranch north of Reno to my other ranch, Bella's Hacienda, in Wells, affords me ample time for meditation and contemplation. Brainstorms grace me during these treks through the high desert, lost in thought.

One Monday morning in January 2019, as I cruised along Interstate 80 across the sagebrush seas and mountain-ringed playas unbroken between the far-flung towns of Fernley and Lovelock, Winnemucca and Battle Mountain, Carlin and Elko, my mind percolated. I would be in residence at Bella's for the next seven days, supervising as madam. *What were my objectives for the week?*

In my mind's eye, I set my intention for Bella's to bring in boom business: for the ladies and the house to make abundant money, and for the customers to thoroughly enjoy themselves. A win-win-win outcome. However, as I drove on through the solitude — the empty miles piling up behind — I realized I was seeking something more. Like a lens zooming out, my consciousness suddenly expanded, from focusing on the smaller, practical picture of how much income would be generated and how many parties realized, to considering the bigger picture:

I've taught my courtesans to be proud and confident about their work. And they should be. *Photo by Brandi Betancourt*

Fostering an attitude shift in the ladies as to how they viewed themselves in their current roles as professional providers of sensual services — and as orchestrators of their own destiny. I wanted them to experience a lesson in taking charge of their lives, their futures.

I resolved that I would use the next seven days to reveal to them what amazing opportunities existed at Bella's Hacienda Ranch. And — in fact — what the ranch *truly* represented.

What it truly represented was a path to *personal empowerment* for the women who worked there. The secret lay in consciously manifesting their dreams.

How to activate this mind shift? The universe swiftly sent me a solution:

I'd use the whiteboard.

OUR FISCAL WEEK AT Bella's Hacienda starts on Sunday and runs through Saturday. Weekends tend to be busiest. Mondays and

Tuesdays typically are slow, Wednesdays and Thursdays show a steady uptick. When I looked over the books that Monday afternoon, I saw there had been just a trickle of business on Sunday, and scant income so far this Monday.

I decided that the morrow would be the day I'd introduce my empowerment concept.

The women eat at a long table in the dining room next to the kitchen. Against one wall stands the giant whiteboard on wheels. One corner of this dry-erase board is reserved for me to write notices to the bartender/hostesses and the working women, such as rules and reminders for the house. Another corner of the board lists the women in residence for the week, and when their blood tests are due to maintain their work cards with the city. Aside from these two corners, the broad swath of the board is left open. In this area, the working women are free to write whatever is on their mind. Maybe they'll post an inspirational quote they've found on social media, or draw a cartoonish figure, using the red, blue or green markers in the bottom tray.

Two weeks before, when I'd been at the ranch for a weeklong residence, I'd suggested the women write their personal goals on the board. "This is an exercise in affirmation, in positive thinking," I'd said at breakfast. "I'd like each of you to write a little statement on the board about what you want to attain. What your big goals are right at this moment. Just be truthful, and sign your name."

They *had*:

"Get fit."

"Better health."

"A new car."

"More abundance."

Now I was prepared to up the ante regarding affirmations. Five courtesans were in the house this week: Lacey, Jade, Mercedes, Rose and Chastity. They ranged in age from twenties to forties, represented a mix of races: white, Asian, African-American.

On Tuesday morning, as they were eating breakfast, I knew the moment was right.

"Ladies," I said, gesturing at the scrawlings on the whiteboard. "Let's think about this. Is this really how you feel this week? I'd like you to think seriously, for just a moment, and be true to yourselves about what your *real* goals are for the near future. Then, if you like, go up and write those goals on the board."

A sexual experience was what we put a price tag on, but that experience would have no value without the comforting attention, warmth and intimacy that the girls were offering.

One by one, they did. Some goals were modest, others ambitious. Jade wrote: "Learn French." Lacey wrote: "A house, land, and good health."

I went last. I wrote a word in big letters above all the affirmations:

EMPOWERMENT.

"*This* is the true purpose of Bella's Hacienda Ranch," I announced. "It's empowering all of you to reach your goals. All that's required is to believe that the ranch is your mechanism for empowerment — and that you can use your work here to make your dreams come true. So, dream big. You can never expand on a little dream. Think about what's *really* in your heart, what your real passions are."

On Wednesday morning, I noted how intent the women were in expressing their goals on the whiteboard. It had become a serious exercise. New goals were scribbled. Other goals were refined. Lacey had reordered her objectives to read: "Good health, a condo, and land." Her consciousness was shifting as a result of putting her desires into writing. It was the same with the other women. Their minds were engaged with their futures.

That, I thought with satisfaction, was one of the keys to empowerment. The workers were investing their intention into dreams. Still, there was another component that was needed. *Intention* is only half the equation. *Attention* — to details — is the other.

I decided to add another dimension to the exercise.

"Let's add some verbiage here," I said, standing at the board during breakfast. "What are we *really* about here at the ranch? What services do we provide? You are giving them much more than sex or a blowjob! What do you think they really need and love about this place?"

It turned out that all the women already had a deep knowingness that they were offering men something more than sex. True, a sexual experience was what we put a price tag on, but that experience would have no value without the comforting attention, warmth and intimacy that the girls were offering. I could tell that this simple exercise in listing what our real offerings were had truly given the women a new take on their own value as individuals, and the work they perform as part of a long human tradition.

By the time they were done listing what they were offering, it really boiled down to simply touching their customers — giving them that comforting attention, warmth and intimacy.

The courtesans, I realized, had, in spirit, joined the elite of their profession: the historic *La Cortigiana Onesta* of Renaissance Italy. They had embraced the providing of sensual services as an esteemed calling, the way that Veronica Franco had in that bygone era.

The payoff soon followed . . .

THE BUSINESS THAT POURED in, beginning on Wednesday, was astounding. The ladies' act of acknowledging what their profession was about proved to be like unlocking and springing open a magic door.

The doorbell rang again and again. It wasn't the quantity of customers the women were suddenly attracting. It was the *kind*. Many of the men who were coming through the door now — in addition to our main staple, truck drivers — had driven up in expensive cars and pickup trucks. Some of them had just won big while gambling in the area's casinos.

That day, Bella's take for the week went from a few hundred dollars brought in so far, to 10 times that. This torrent of revenue was money the women were splitting evenly with the house. Their share would help move them toward the goals they'd written on the whiteboard. And they were realizing this flood of income by proudly and confidently providing the exact services our guests wanted and needed. Services rendered in the spirit of *La Cortigiana Onesta*.

The phenomenon they were a part of this week was the pure manifesting of their dreams.

ONE OF MY RITUALS at the ranch at the time was making a run each morning to Bella's Restaurant & Espresso, a five-minute drive away, to grab a cup of Americano. I was excited to see the restaurant was doing boom business this week, too. Thursday, Friday and Saturday, the restaurant was packed. I could never have orchestrated that. It was all divine: some sort of cosmic echo of the positive energy unleashed at the ranch.

At the ranch, morale was high. The courtesans and bartenders were buzzing with excitement. The women realized how much money was walking through the door, and they linked it to their affirmations on the whiteboard. Their attitude had grown assured, expectant. My lesson in manifesting had hit home. They had come around to understanding that they could empower themselves to attract customers and dollars *if* they put the correct thoughts and energy behind their intentions, and followed through with attention to detail — doing the best they were able, while interacting with customers, and completely avoiding or overriding the typical negative thought patterns of feeling like victims, and of concocting excuses for failures or droughts.

The signs out front spell out services as clear as day. *Photo by Jason Kelley*

Cause and effect. They acknowledged that they, *themselves*, were responsible for the consequences of their actions.

Success was all up to them.

And, my goodness, were they enjoying success. The money just kept flowing. It was like nothing the courtesans had ever seen at Bella's. They'd never experienced this kind of plentitude. Wednesday had been good, but the pace picked up significantly on Thursday, and carried on even stronger on Friday, as we enjoyed what I call "the double digits" of revenue. That is, revenue that was well into the five figures — two-digit numerals followed by three zeros.

Several customers had booked overnight parties in which they paid extra to share a bed all night with a courtesan, waking up with her in the morning. These customers would get up at 5:30 or 6 in the morning and walk into the bar for a cup of coffee, then be on their way. Or not on their way. Some stayed for even more pleasure.

The pages of our ledger were filling up with nonstop bookings.

NOW IT WAS 4:30 p.m. Saturday. I'd begun my shift as on-floor manager, tending bar and answering the door. The phone in the bar rang. The other bartender answered it.

"Yes, she's here," she said into the receiver, and handed it to me.

It was Marixa, the young waitress at the restaurant. This was unusual, her calling me at the ranch. Her tone was earnest.

"Remember, a few weeks ago, this man sat at your table?" she began. "I think it was you and a friend. Well, he was asking to see you. So, I just wanted to see if you were there."

I empathized with Gavin's plight. His wish for waking up — just once— with a woman beside him in bed stuck in my head. There has to be a way.

I shuffled through my memory banks. Who had joined me at the table at the restaurant in the past few weeks? Was it John, one of our regulars? He'd sat and chatted with me at the restaurant before. No, it couldn't have been John. I hadn't seen him in a good long while ...

Then a face flashed:

Gavin.

Gavin is a truck driver. He's driven a semi most of his adult life. I've known him for probably two decades, since he was in his thirties. He pops into the ranch now and then. He is super nice, but lacking in self-confidence when it comes to romance. In his youth, he'd contracted a mild muscular disorder. As a result, he has a bit of a gimpy gait; one of his legs turns in a bit, and his shoulders move unevenly. He also lisps and slurs his words because his tongue doesn't cooperate fully. But these are very minor disabilities. His speech is entirely understandable, and his standing posture is straight. In fact, he's pleasant looking — 6-feet-plus in height, slender in build, blond haired — and fun to be around because of his good nature. His lack of self-assurance in dating is unfortunate. So far, he seems resigned to being single.

I remembered that a few weeks before as I was sitting in the restaurant with one of my friends, I'd spied Gavin sitting in a nearby booth. He'd walked over and asked if he could join us. It turned out he patronized the restaurant somewhat regularly. I hadn't known that.

Gavin had told a few colorful but very cute jokes. Then his talk turned personal.

"You know, Bella," he'd said, "before I die, I want to wake up with a woman — but for no money. That's never happened."

Here he was, past his 50th birthday.

"Gavin," I'd said, "it's never your physical form that determines whether you pay or never pay. You pay, because we *all* pay. In some kind of physical, mental or spiritual coin. Maybe the monetary coin is the easiest one to pay in."

His mouth had formed a little smile.

"You know, Bella, when I get to the pearly gates, God and I are going to have a talk. I got a question for Him: 'What did *I* do?'"

He'd laughed a hearty chuckle. He certainly was a sweet man.

I empathized with his plight. Gavin's wish for waking up — just once — with a woman beside him in bed stuck in my head. His situation kept popping into my consciousness over the next couple weeks. My mind began working on it, as minds do when presented with a puzzle.

There has *to be a way . . .*

Gavin's face kept passing through my mind during this week at the ranch. Here we were, enjoying copious bookings. And now, this call from Marixa.

Talk about synchronicity!

"Oh, that was Gavin," I told her. "Tell him to come on over."

We'd been so busy Saturday afternoon, I needed to restock the bar with beer. I hurried out back to the walk-in cooler. When I returned with a case, Gavin was sitting there. He hadn't wasted any time after Marixa had informed him that I was at the ranch.

I gave him a hug. I hug all the customers. And they are genuine hugs, from my heart. I locked Gavin in an extra-long embrace.

We chitchatted a bit. Then I popped the question:

"Well, are you going to date?"

I leaned in close, lowered my voice and grinned. "How about that overnight?"

"Oh," Gavin said. "How much would that cost?"

"I don't know. You've got to talk to the lady!"

Right about then, Lacey walked in after finishing a party.

Let me tell you Lacey's story . . .

Courtesans can graduate to bartending and managing. *Photo by Victory Tischler-Blue*

LACEY HAS BEEN WITH me off and on over eight years. She has brown hair and a voluptuous figure with a thin waist: legitimately hour-glassed: 38-30-32. And — to quote from her profile on the ranch's website — she is "very open minded."

Lacey is a Florida native. In her time out West, she gradually lost her lilting drawl, but she resurrects it, as needed, in role playing. Her boudoir skills are extremely developed. Lacey can play the part of a dominatrix, complete with leather outfit, belts and whips, or the submissive. Tell her your fantasy or fetish, she'll fulfill it.

(Note to reader: Lacey has shared her story and thoughts in this book's bonus section, "Courtesans' Stories — in Their Own Words.")

Lacey had been gone from the brothel for about a year when she'd showed up in 2017 with a new partner in tow. His name was Cleve. He was gaunt and wheezy. My heart went out to her. Lacey was several months pregnant. They were destitute.

"Belle," she'd said, using her nickname for me, "I didn't know where else we could go where we'd be safe."

I could only imagine the rough living they'd been through!

I set them up in a room at the brothel across from mine. I put Lacey on the daytime bartender shift. When she'd worked for me before, she'd had work cards both for bartending and sex work. The bartending card was good for three years before renewal. I hired Cleve as a waiter at Bella's Restaurant & Espresso. He struggled. The work was too physically demanding. He had advanced COPD, possibly from cigarettes or abusing hard drugs.

Lacey hinted to me about Cleve's hard-living past. He was 40, just a few years older than she, but looked much older. They'd met in Las Vegas and fallen in love. Then they'd gotten into some trouble and had to leave in a hurry. They'd come to me.

She and Cleve were starting a new family, and intended to get married. Lacey ended up giving birth in the hospital in Elko. They named the baby boy Cleve Jr. They packed up and left for Indiana, where Cleve Sr. had family.

Now, at the start of this new year, Lacey was back at Bella's. Her sister in Florida was watching Cleve Jr. while Lacey worked a while at Bella's. Cleve Sr. was dead. Lacey had crawled into bed next to him one night, and curled up to a corpse.

Fast forward to the week of bounty I've been describing. I visited with Lacey on Tuesday morning.

"How are you doing, dear?" I'd asked.

"Well, Belle, I'm really angry."

She was mad at her late partner. She was working through the dark phases of grief.

I was proud of Lacey. She was fulfilling the mission of the house, the calling of the true courtesan. *Touch. Comfort. Intimacy.* The bargain she was offering was akin to a random act of kindness.

We talked it out.

"Well, why would you be upset with him?" I asked.

That opened the floodgate. She unburdened her heart.

"Belle, why wasn't I strong enough? Why didn't I see it? I should have known better!"

"You're never angry with *him*," I said gently. "You're angry with *you*. You haven't forgiven *you* for falling in love with someone who had real problems, and didn't even let on that maybe he was still using."

She stared into space. "I've been around long enough, Belle. I should have seen it. I should have known. I should have gotten out."

"Forgive yourself," I said softly. "If you were supposed to have known, you would have known."

She burst into tears. She nodded. She was forgiving herself.

And from that moment on, the money started pouring in for her at the house.

It was pouring in for *all* the women. A mysterious force was at work at Bella's.

And now, Gavin had showed up. Lacey sat at the bar next to him and smiled. They started talking. The doorbell rang. I greeted the new customer and pressed the buzzer behind the bar to signal the women to come out to the parlor to form a lineup. When I returned to the bar, Gavin was alone.

I walked back to the bedrooms and found Lacey.

"Lacey, this is what I know about Gavin," I began — and shared his dream about waking up with a woman.

The story moved her deeply.

Lacey returned to the bar and picked up where she'd left off with Gavin. I overheard her offering him a real deal: a 12-hour party for $1,500. That was the price a skilled courtesan could command for a one-hour party at Bella's. It was 5 p.m. and Gavin would have her until 5 a.m. *And* on the busiest night of the week — when she could have booked one party after another.

I was proud of Lacey. She was fulfilling the mission of the house, the calling of the true courtesan. *Touch. Comfort. Intimacy.* The bargain she was offering was akin to a random act of kindness. It was in line with manifesting, the theme of the week. One effect would be its continuing the flow of customers through our doors, the stream of revenue into our pockets. But, most of all, Lacey felt the offer in her heart. She was committed to helping Gavin realize his dream.

I kept an eye on the two of them. I could see he was warming to the prospect. He was going to run his credit card. But he kept frowning. I knew why.

The money. It didn't square with how he'd envisioned his fantasy.

I slid his credit card into our machine at the bar.

The transaction was rejected. The requested sum had exceeded his daily withdrawal limit. He was only able to get $500.

Lacey brought him back to her room. They had an hour-long party.

When they returned, I could tell something had changed in Gavin. As they sat at the bar, he turned to her and said, "Lacey, I'm going to the truck stop. If I come back, I'll have the money. If I don't come back, you'll know I couldn't get the money."

He headed off to one of the truck stops in town.

Around 10 p.m., Gavin returned. He bought Lacey a couple drinks at the bar. I poured them. He was smiling a bit now, between those frowns.

He nodded at Lacey. "You know, my intention is to do the overnight. You must have a great poker face."

Her casual expression vanished. She peered into his eyes. Her voice lowered.

"Gavin, I lost the man I love. He died. I *would like* to wake up next to you."

Gavin was startled. "You're sincere! You *would* really like to wake up next to me."

"Yes. I would really like that."

She led him back to her room.

LACEY SHARED THIS WITH me on Sunday morning, after Gavin had left:

"He didn't want me to hold him. I had no problem sleeping next to him. When he woke up and opened his eyes and saw me laying next to him, the smile on his face is one I'll remember my whole life."

I could envision that smile. And I could imagine the sweet scene Gavin would remember the rest of his life: waking up and looking at this beautiful woman lying next to him, who wanted to be there with him.

I preach female empowerment and financial independence at Bella's. *Photo by Brandi Betancourt*

Lacey told me more. She'd helped him shower — washing him, doing the comforting things she wanted to do — and it had given her gratification way beyond the dollar amount.

She'd walked him to the front door and given him a huge hug. It was around 6 a.m., about an hour before full sunrise.

Gavin then said this to her: "Do you know how hard it's gonna be to drive past this place in two days and not stop?"

Before walking out into the pinkness of dawn, he'd shaken his head slowly and said one last thing:

"I'll probably stop."

SATURDAY NIGHT AT BELLA'S had been one for the books. So had the entire week. It had all begun with the courtesans writing out their dreams on the whiteboard, then revising them as the week progressed.

I had set this outcome into motion on my drive to Wells on Monday: aligning my intention to manifest a big week at the ranch by guiding the ladies toward manifesting their personal destinies. I had spurred them to jot down their dreams on the whiteboard, so they could convert those ambitions into self-fulfilling prophesies.

If the results of this bountiful week were any proof, the ladies were on the right path. It had been a great learning experience for them — and validation for me about the power of positive thinking.

I spend some bonding moments with courtesans in the backroom lounge. *Photo by Victory Tischler-Blue*

I viewed it all with a Zen approach. The men who'd come in all had arrived at their correct times, left at their correct times, and had the correct amount of money to spend in order for the whole week to play out correctly. The customers had come, and come, and come. And one of them, Gavin, had seen a once-in-a-lifetime desire fulfilled.

It all had been confirmation to me about the philosophy I embraced: Whatever you put your *intention* on, as long as you put your *attention* on it, will manifest.

I trusted the ladies understood.

That Sunday morning, as they ate breakfast, I had one more thought to share with them about posting their affirmations on the whiteboard.

"Think about using your real names on the whiteboard, when writing your dreams and goals."

I explained that the house names they were using were the names of the personas they adopted at Bella's. The persona was the facilitator of the courtesan's income, rather than the actual person, the real person within.

It was the actual person who would benefit from the income and use it to attain her goals.

I spoke to Lacey. "'Lacey' has no past or future. Now *Linda*, on the other hand, she wants to keep fit, have the good vibes, own the condo. You could have the wrong name here. 'Lacey' is the facilitator of your money. Linda is supposed to stay out of the way."

She laughed and stood up from the table. "You're right, Belle," she said.

Under her affirmation, she erased "Lacey" and replaced it with "Linda," her real name.

"Now, think about it," I continued. "All those working-lady names on the board. 'Mercedes' doesn't want to learn French. *Ashlee* wants to learn French. "'Mercedes' is the facilitator of the money so that Ashlee can go do whatever she wants to do."

In turn, they each switched their persona names with their real names.

"You know, Belle?" Lacey/Linda said. "As soon as you put that empowerment word on the board, it all happened."

Before I left, I wrote, "Bella" on the board with this affirmation: "The brothel creates the money that allows everyone involved to meet their dreams and goals."

Lacey/Linda said goodbye to me at the entrance.

"Belle, you have such a big presence. I'd like to be able to duplicate it and manifest."

I hugged her.

"If everyone will do exactly what I guided them to do, this place *will* manifest," I said.

ON MY MARATHON DRIVE back to Reno that day, another revelation popped into my mind: I was fulfilling my calling as a

21st century madam. Bella's was part of an evolution of the sensual-services industry in modern civilization — harkening back to *La Cortigiana Onesta*.

My ranch was a testing ground for the empowerment to be realized by professional providers of sensual services. What had transpired at Bella's Hacienda over the week that had passed is what needs to happen on a daily basis in every licensed house, in order for the brothel industry to move forward.

I thought back, again, to Gavin and Lacey. Their overnight party had been an absolute awakening and healing for both people: one a dreamer, one a griever.

It came to me that an awakening for humanity as a whole is in order. And I experienced an epiphany: The reason I'd owned Bella's for so long was meant to be part of a grander purpose. A mission loomed for me. I wasn't clear on the specifics of what this grand mission would be. I only knew it had to do with revolutionizing the brothel industry. This would mean bringing it out of the Dark Ages as a whole, changing society's regard for it here in America, and around the world. It would ultimately mean legalizing the providing of sex for pay in every possible jurisdiction.

It eventually came to me that what is needed is a strong, consistent, coordinated movement worldwide to humanize the sex-for-sale industry — to transform it into a legitimate and respectable sector of society in every civilized land. The vast benefits of this revolutionary change would be enormous for the human race even beyond the health, safety and economic dividends by normalizing and regulating transactional sex.

If you accept the premise that a root cause of a great deal of destructive anti-social behavior is a lack of emotional and sexual fulfillment for the perpetrators, then imagine how making professional sex-for-hire accessible to adults could prove to be a safety valve. And for visitors to a brothel who are not criminally minded, the services to be had can prove extremely therapeutic, making them happier, more productive people.

Granted, mental health is extremely complex. There is no panacea — not even psychotherapy or anti-depressants — for curing every form of profound psychological problem. But I do know that a large number of the customers who come to Bella's do so because they are seeking interactions they can't seem to find elsewhere. Men like Gavin. And they are no different from patrons of legal sex-for-hire throughout history.

In various eras, government leaders have openly recognized the importance of legal brothels. I mentioned several of them in Chapter Three. One was Solon, the Athenian statesmen who lived approximately 630-560 B.C., and reputedly instituted Athens' first brothels, earmarking the earnings to building a temple to Aphrodite. According to a writing of contemporary Greek playwright Philemon, Solon's establishment of brothels was to "democratize" the accessibility of sexual pleasure.

Jumping ahead nine centuries or so, the influential Christian theologian Augustine of Hippo (A.D. 354-430), was quoted thusly: "If you expel prostitution from society, you will unsettle everything on account of lusts." That view was echoed an additional nine centuries later by Catholic priest and theologian Thomas Aquinas (A.D. 1225-74), who said, "If prostitution were to be suppressed, careless lusts would overthrow society."

And here we are today, in the third decade of the 21st century, with the need greater than ever for a global, humanizing transformation of the sex industry.

It is my mission to play a catalytic role in this sexual evolution.

Courtesans take shifts broadcasting greetings and invitations to Interstate 80 truckers over the CB radio. *Photo by Victory Tischler-Blue*

CHAPTER SEVEN

Frank Talk with Sex Workers On the Prospect of Legalization

The prospect of widespread decriminalization of transactional sex is gradually growing in the United States. It's occurring imperceptibly to the vast majority. But signs of this legal and cultural shift have emerged clearly in my field of vision.

My eyes widen when I read about proposed legislation to change the legal status of sex work in states such as New York and Vermont, Massachusetts and Maine, and in Washington, D.C. My ears perk up at the public comments of elected officials reported by mainstream media. My mind percolates as it detects — behind the headlines of these stories — the subtle hand of history at play. And my imagination kicks in, considering these questions:

Once bills to decriminalize sex for pay make it into the lawbooks in these jurisdictions, can legalized sex-for-pay be far behind?

Is my vision for the legalization of Nevada-style brothels all across our country be inching closer to reality?

Decriminalization is, of course, different from legalization. The former is the reduction of criminal penalizations when someone commits an illegal act. The latter is the lack of legal prohibitions of an act. But the tiny glints of decriminalization on the far horizon are, to me, harbingers of the eventual wide-scale legalization of transactional sex in the United States. And history backs my conviction. I am, after all, a Nevadan — and my perspective is shaped by how Nevada's live-and-let-live ethos has influenced the rest of the nation.

The Silver State, as I write these words, is the only state in the Union with a measure of legalized transactional sex. And it is noteworthy that Nevada has consistently been a pioneer in legalizing activities the rest of the states had outlawed, only to have other states eventually follow our lead. Throughout its existence, Nevada has earned the unofficial nickname of "the Maverick State." Given its harsh climate and boom-or-bust mining industry, Nevada's political and economic leaders have periodically primed the state's economy by audaciously legalizing industries that are banned elsewhere. These activities include prizefighting (in 1897), quickie divorces (with six-week residencies) and casino gambling (both in 1931), and recreational marijuana (in 2017). Inevitably, other states have followed suit.

Will this hold true for legalizing brothels? Consider the following:

- In 2022, bills to decriminalize prostitution were being considered in both the Senate and the Assembly of New York state's Legislature to repeal statutes criminalizing sex work between consenting adults and to provide criminal-record relief for those convicted of crimes repealed under the bills. The justification by supporters of the New York bills was typical of those backing similar legislation elsewhere: to abolish the stigma of consensual adult sex for pay and its illegitimacy that can leave sex workers vulnerable to being victimized by assault and coercion (including sex trafficking) — as they would be reluctant to report these crimes to police — as well as put them at risk of losing certain legal protections. (As examples, tenants convicted of prostitution offenses can face eviction; job seekers with such convictions on their record can be denied employment.)

- In 2020, Vermont's Legislature considered a bill similar to New York's.

- In 2021, Maine's governor signed into law a bill that prevents conviction of a person selling sex if the person did so to "prevent bodily injury, serious economic hardship or another threat to the person or another person."
- Also in 2021, Massachusetts state lawmakers considered a bill that would repeal the selling and buying of sex between consenting adults, and would repeal the crime of so-called "common nightwalking."
- In 2019, councilmembers of the District of Columbia considered but rejected a bill that would have made Washington, D.C., the first U.S. city to decriminalize prostitution.

What these bills underscore is that here in the 2020s, we are seeing stirrings by political leaders outside of Nevada who are opening their minds, and mouths, to the possibility that decriminalizing the oldest profession — in a safe, and regulated way — would have benefits far outweighing any potential detriments. Elected officials favoring such legislation have come to terms with the fact that continuing to treat transactional sex as taboo does not help society.

As evidence that the discourse is much broader than regional — in fact, national — in scope, consider what I pointed out in Chapter Three about the stated views of two of the leading Democratic contenders in the 2020 presidential race. Pete Buttigieg, a former mayor of South Bend, Indiana (and later the U.S. secretary of transportation), said that the subject of sex work, and I quote, "needs to be part of a larger conversation about how we treat sex workers and all of the reasons why this society hesitates to embrace the idea of sex work." Another leading 2020 Democratic contender — then-U.S. Sen. Kamala Harris of California (and subsequently U.S. vice president) — had gone on the record in 2019, in an interview with *The Root* (a news-and-culture website dedicated to reporting on African-American issues), that she conditionally supports decriminalization of transactional sex. Harris said, in part, "when you're talking about consenting adults, I think that yes we should really consider that we can't criminalize consensual behavior as long as no one is being harmed."

As I also pointed out in Chapter Three, this view has already been embraced by governments on six continents. In their nations, transactional sex enjoys limited legality in various jurisdictions. My personal campaign is to promote the legalization of Nevada-style brothels across the United States. I shared copious reasons in Chapter Four supporting this stance.

IN THIS CHAPTER, I am sharing perceptions and opinions from a variety of sex workers, themselves, about the pros, cons and likelihood of Nevada-style brothels being legalized outside of Nevada. Their viewpoints are critical to this discourse. After all, they represent the pool of people who would likely be working in this newly minted industry.

I facilitated interviews on this subject with nine sex workers — asking what advantages and disadvantages they see in the Nevada model for brothels, whether they favor its adoption in other states, and whether they believe it *will* be adopted. While their opinions (and backgrounds) vary, almost all of them support the spread of legal Nevada-style brothels. But they are less sure when, or if, this could happen.

At the time of these interviews in late 2022, four of these sex workers had never worked in a brothel. The other five had done stints at Bella's, yet also worked illegally — meaning, they performed transactional sex in violation of the law — before working at my legal brothel. Following are their perspectives — which I provide along with a bit of background on each.

I must also note that these interviews were arranged with the ground rule that these women's identities would be protected. Therefore, the names used below are not their real names. Certain other identifying details were omitted.

I'll start with the four women who've never worked in a brothel.

Foxxy: Legalizing transactional sex would provide safe options to strippers who already cross the line in clubs

FOXXY KNOWS WHAT TRANSPIRES in the private VIP rooms at strip clubs such as the one she's worked at in San Francisco. And she knows that exotic dancers keen on doing lucrative "extras" by accepting dates with customers outside the club can make a fair amount of additional income.

"It's very well known in my club that the older women — late thirties, early forties — are essentially full-service sex workers," says the pixie-featured 20-year-old with buzz-cut dyed-blond hair, dark-blue eyes and the lean, lithe body of a trained ballet dancer.

She, herself, has occasionally violated her club's rules (not to mention, local and state laws) against performing sex acts such as hand jobs and blow jobs in the VIP rooms to secure bigger tips. And she's accepted invitations from a handful of guests to visit them in their hotel rooms for sex.

Even though transactional sex remains criminalized in every U.S. state, with the exception of legal brothels in Nevada, the sex-for-pay trade is growing surreptitiously in legitimate establishments such as strip clubs, Foxxy says. And she sees merit in changing laws to allow legal sex in strip clubs for dancers who want to go that route, by creating a hybrid strip club/brothel where boundaries currently legally off limits can be negotiated by the dancers and clients.

"I would love to see that happen in the exotic-dancing industry, because nine times out of ten, the people who come into a club come in with the expectation of sex acts," she says. "When you're signing up to be a stripper and do this type of work, what your job really is, is to provide a fantasy. It's professional teasing."

Two years earlier, Foxxy never would have thought about being a professional teaser — much less getting paid thousands of dollars for under-the-table sex acts. But here she is, supporting herself and investing her savings as an exotic dancer who occasionally provides "extras."

Foxxy ventured into stripping after her professional path as a ballet dancer was cut short by a career-ending back injury. It was a hard detour from her dreams of becoming a ballerina she'd nurtured from an early age, growing up in the Baltimore area. Her parents had put her in dance lessons at age 4. By the time she was 12, her family was making sacrifices of time and money to ensure their daughter had solid training to pursue her passion.

At 18, Foxxy auditioned for a prestigious apprenticeship with a renowned ballet company in San Francisco. She beat out more than 1,000 applicants for one of the few coveted slots. Before moving cross-country, she saved money waitressing to support her living expenses in pricy San Francisco. Her parents agreed to cover half the rent she paid — sharing a one-bedroom apartment with two fellow apprenticing dancers — as long as she progressed toward a college degree, taking online courses.

However, before her first year in the apprenticeship ended, Foxxy's career aspirations came to a crushing crash due to a lingering lower-back injury she'd sustained at 17. The rigorous workouts of the apprenticeship exacerbated the strain. One day, during a rehearsal, "I landed wrong, and I just felt something kind of tweak," she recalls. Foxxy found herself on the floor, unable to stand.

The diagnosis was nerve damage. A doctor warned she had to quit ballet if she wanted to continue walking. Foxxy was devastated. Her self-identity had been bound up with dance. "It was as if someone died," she says. With her parents pushing her to finish her degree, Foxxy found herself at a crossroads. She wasn't interested in working in her academic field. She saw herself as an *entertainer*.

"I was kind of at a loss. I went home for Thanksgiving break. I saw one of my close friends from high school. It turned out she'd been stripping for six months. She was in an abusive relationship. I agreed to drop her off and pick her up from her club, instead of her boyfriend. The

CHAPTER SEVEN

Ebony and Ivory. Two courtesans can readily fulfill a guest's request for a *ménage à trois*. Photo by Brandi Betancourt

first night I picked her up, she was counting out her money for the night, and it all kind of came together seamlessly in my mind. I needed a job that paid a lot of money because I was tired of relying on other people financially. I thought, 'This is my ticket. This is how I keep performing, how I stay on stage. This is a good transition for me. And I'm only going to do it over Christmas break, in Baltimore. I'm not going to do it in San Francisco, because frankly, I don't want to be walking through the Tenderloin with bags of cash every night.'"

Clad in a skimpy top and a mini-dress, pasties and six-inch stripper heels, Foxxy auditioned at her friend's club. "I couldn't climb on the pole and do tricks, because you need to learn how to do that, but I was fine on stage."

As she worked the 9 p.m. to 3 a.m. shift, collecting $20 and $100 bills, Foxxy handled even the shadiest customers fine, too. "There were dealers coming in and out, and there were a lot of pedophiles coming into that club," Foxxy says. "Some of them have a savior complex, like a Richard Gere in *Pretty Woman* type thing. 'Little girl, you're too pretty to be here. What are you doing here? I could take you out of this. I'll support you.'" Her reply to them was simple: "I don't do that."

Foxxy worked a few more shifts after returning home for Christmas break, clearing $500 one night after tipping out the house mom (dressing-room manager), DJ and security guard. Back in San Francisco, one of her roommates who worked at Trader Joe's helped Foxxy get hired there. But with the feeling fresh in her mind of the cash she'd made at the Baltimore club, Foxxy successfully auditioned at a San Francisco club near Chinatown that catered to high-end guests.

"I made twelve hundred on my first night, a Saturday night," she remembers. The manager gave her a trial by fire, repeatedly sending her into a VIP room, set behind a one-way glass mirror, where well-heeled customers order expensive bottle service and are known to offer to pay dancers for activities beyond those legally permissible. Unbeknownst to Foxxy, the manager was testing how she'd handle a particular club regular who was known to corrupt new girls.

The man — a rich, flabby, balding contract attorney in his fifties — was perched on a plush couch. After Foxxy exited after the half-hour party, the manager quizzed her: "So what did you guys do?" Foxxy explained how disgusting the customer was, reeking of rotten garlic, and that she'd turned down his requests to kiss his neck and hairy chest. The manager was pleased she hadn't been a pushover.

Foxxy left the club at 4 a.m., rushed home, scrubbed off her makeup, changed into her Trader Joe's uniform, grabbed a quick bite, caught the bus to work and started her shift at 6 a.m.

"I was stocking shelves and having flashbacks to a thousand dollars being handed to me," she says. "I worked there three hours, told them I was feeling sick, left and never went back."

In time, Foxxy mastered tricks on the pole. But most of the money she's made has not been from getting tipped on stage or being paid to perform lap dances at tables, but in servicing wealthy guests — including couples — in the VIP rooms, where the base fee is $500 for a half-hour of a dancer's time, and it's common for guests to tip the dancer a matching amount, as well as keeping the clock running for additional half-hours. As Foxxy quickly learned, some dancers were willing to do hand jobs and blow jobs on VIP customers for extra compensation. They got away with it by tipping out the VIP hosts — security guards — so they would refrain from entering the room to monitor for taboo behavior.

Foxxy explains that while strip clubs in jurisdictions such as Baltimore County may have undercover vice detectives coming in — looking to bust anyone violating sex laws — it's different in San Francisco, where strippers worry less about cops and more about "shoppers": shills sent by the clubs' corporate owners to catch strippers violating company policy. She says she knew to be careful about accepting such parties, and in fact, rarely does. When a customer asks, "What do I get?" she'll answer coyly. "If you come right out and say, 'I'm not sucking your dick,' they're not going to take you upstairs. I say, 'Oh, you *have* to find out. It's a good time. It's a private dance.' I've learned to be a little more forthcoming about what my boundaries are. I'll say, 'If you're not into it, there are other girls who will do what you want.'"

And there *are*, Foxxy says.

Her boundaries, however, mean rejecting just about any male customer who wants more than a grinding lap dance, or who puts his hands where they don't belong "I don't let people go anywhere near my vagina, not with their hands, not with their face, not under my clothes, not over my clothes. We're not technically allowed to be topless in the rooms. I'll go topless for the tip that I ask for, which is equal to the price of the room. It'll be a full lap dance, with grinding. They can touch me anywhere where there is not already clothing, except for my tits. They can grab my ass."

She'll loosen her boundaries for certain female guests, however. Foxxy's sexual orientation is lesbian.

"I have more of a sexually ambiguous appearance than most of the girls in the club, and sometimes I'll get couples, and they'll take two girls, all of us in one room, and the guy will go with the other girl and the woman will go with me," she says. "Two or three times, I have done oral sex on the woman, because that's something I feel comfortable with doing. And the couples were obviously millionaires, and very clean."

One such couple took Foxxy and another girl into a VIP room. The man then offered Foxxy $2,000 to visit them at their room in a luxury hotel in town, to perform oral sex on his fiancée. "They were getting married soon, and he wanted to do something nice for her." Foxxy took the rare gig, which violates club policy about seeing guests outside the club. However, being a good earner in the club gives her a bit of protection to have managers ignore suspicions she might be doing outcalls, she says.

"I charge two grand for going out to dinner. I charge five grand for a longer night, and they don't necessarily involve sex. I've had sex for money less times than I can count on my hands. I charge two thousand to three thousand, and it's mostly been with women."

Foxxy was, however, willing to make an exception with a tall, handsome professional athlete who paid her to give him a hand job in a VIP room. After the party, he asked her for her phone number, which she provided.

When he left the club without tipping her the amount he'd promised, she was peeved. Then she got a call from him when she was leaving work, telling her he'd text her the address for the hotel. "He didn't end up texting it to me. I think he just kind of got cold feet."

Foxxy had his name from his credit card. She Googled the name and learned he was "a pretty big deal" in the Major Leagues as a star pitcher. Evidently, he was in San Francisco because his team was playing the Giants. She also discovered he was engaged to his longtime girlfriend: a beautiful social-media influencer. The pair's beaming faces, in fact, were posted on various websites, portraying them as a beautiful couple.

A month later, Foxxy was on vacation for her birthday with a girlfriend, to whom she'd told about the cheating cheapskate ballplayer who'd stiffed her. "I got pretty drunk, and she kind of like egged me on to message his girlfriend on Instagram and tell her," Foxxy says. So Foxxy did, explaining that the woman's fiancé had been in the strip club about a month ago. "I said we did a private dance, and he told me he was single, and I didn't think much of it, and I didn't really know who he was. I said we had manual sex and made out, and that he'd asked me to come to his hotel room to have sex with him for money."

The response to her IG message was swift: from the *ballplayer*.

"I immediately got a call from him. I think what happened is he's logged into her social accounts. I didn't answer the phone, but that account blocked me, and he blocked me."

The experience illustrated to Foxxy that even men with fame and fortune, good looks and a beautiful partner can have a penchant to stray.

Sex work, she understands, is a huge market.

"The twisted reality of it is that guys come into the club looking for blow jobs or sex, and it's twenty times more expensive than if they go down to the pier and get a hooker. But to them, it's higher class and not 'prostitution' if it's in a strip club. It's in a nice facility. There's security. And you're not going to be busted by a cop."

Therefore, a legal sex club that combines the best elements of a strip club and brothel — to provide workers and customers options — would make sense, Foxxy says. It would legitimize actions already transpiring in the club or arranged by some of the exotic dancers with guests to take place outside the club.

"The way that my club works, on paper there's no sex acts. But if you are in good standing with the club — if you are filling people's pockets adequately — everyone looks the other way."

Foxxy does foresee drawbacks to the combination gentleman's club/bordellos of the future. They would take away the income from illegal sex workers, primarily minorities, who rely on the trade in impoverished areas, she says, and the ownership of these legal sex houses would likely by corporations enriching wealthy male capitalists — who would unfairly exploit the working women.

"In theory, a business that uses women as commodities, being fairly run by men, sounds great, but it never works in practice. There will always be corruption," she says.

"The danger of brothels becoming more mainstream is the bastardization of the model by greedy people with bad intentions. You look at the cannabis industry. It started as street dealing, mostly by people of color. And now you have these huge dispensaries, these huge marijuana companies owned by greedy white businessmen. They're bastardizing the original intent of legalizing marijuana, which was to give an alternate form of healing, or provide something that is recreational. Now you're harming the communities that were originally prospering off this market.

"That is the worry I have for even decriminalizing prostitution. It's going to be gentrified. In some ways it's going to be safer for the girls and the customers. I fear that when there are legal brothels, the women who were working street corners are not going to meet the bar of women being hired, and then they're going to be out of work."

* * *

Lady La sees Nevada-style brothels spreading nationwide in the next two decades as more tolerant Gen Z'ers gain clout

TO LADY LA, IT'S a no-brainer that Nevada-style brothels should be legalized nationwide.

For one reason, they would create secure working conditions for the working women. "Having somebody watching or knowing where you are is really important," the 23-year-old says. "When I did my sugar-baby work, it was dangerous. I feel that's a much safer situation for women."

For another reason, "Everybody should be able to make their own decisions for themselves," she says. "Not that I would want to work in one. One reason why not, I wouldn't want the government to be involved in my money with sex work. But for other people, that should be their decision."

For yet another reason, not adopting the Nevada model for legal brothels won't do anything to prevent transactional sex. Physical sex workers — whether escorts, streetwalkers or sugar babies — "are everywhere," Lady La says. "The market's too big."

'Lady La' says it's a no-brainer that Nevada-style brothels should be legalized nationwide. "Having somebody watching or knowing where you are is really important. When I did my sugar-baby work, it was dangerous.'

The entrepreneurial Lady La — the handle she uses for sex work — has transactional-sex experience both in person and remotely. Blond and petite, with Nordic features and a go-go dancer's level of fitness, she is a hard worker, modeling at promo events and taking dancing gigs. The northern Nevada native also has earned steady income from sex work, but only with one client did it involve the physical act. He was her sugar daddy for six months. The rest of her sex work has been through online camming and web platforms on which she sells racy photos of herself, as well as worn undergarments such as bras or panties, leggings and thigh-high go-go stockings, mailing them to fetishists.

"I have had one sugar daddy in person," she says. "I met him on Tinder when I was eighteen. I was on the app looking for successful men. I had graduated high school, and I was planning on getting married, having a baby with my fiancé. He was only making sixteen an hour at the time, in construction. I wanted something I could do where I could make good money fast. I wanted to buy a car and cover the rent and build up my savings for a down payment for a house. I met a guy who was around forty and he looked like he had a lot of money. It was very nerve wracking meeting him the first time. I didn't know if he was going to have a gun or have other guys there with him. All I had was a little knife.

I couldn't tell anybody, so I didn't have anybody I was checking in with."

The man turned out to be a legitimate client, though not physically appealing. "He wasn't that fat, but he was very hairy. Meeting up with him was definitely uncomfortable. It took a lot of getting used to for me. We always met at a hotel. It was very discreet. It turned out he was married. I don't know what his business status was, but I know he had a lot of money.

"I always messaged him on a texting app. He never had my phone number or my name. I saw him about once a week. He paid me two thousand dollars a month. I was his sugar baby for about six months. It did affect me mentally, sleeping with him. It's a lot for any human to project themselves into something that they don't really want to do. I was in that situation. I wanted the money, but I didn't want to do *that*. Also, I was always worried that my fiancé was going to find out. That's why I stopped. I went ghost. I've never seen him since."

Now married with a small child, Lady La doesn't intend to be a sugar baby again. Yet she enjoys a remote form of sex work she's transitioned into: "doing sugar-baby type work virtually." She had been selling clothes she no longer wanted on Facebook Marketplace. An idea to sell once-worn lingerie to fetishists germinated after she began posting photos of herself on that e-commerce platform, modeling leggings or shoes. She began getting messages from men asking to buy photos of her wearing the items — or to buy the items themselves.

Realizing these men had a yen for obtaining clothes a sexy woman had worn, Lady La decided to start selling once-worn undergarments to these fetishists who contacted her. She gained loyal followers — mostly men, but also a few women, including transgender woman. They apparently crave the smell of her sweat and perfume and the knowledge the items she ships them have clad her flesh.

"I can charge them whatever I want," Lady La says. "Some panties I may sell for fifty dollars, or even eighty dollars, each. It really depends on the person. And if they want the panties, I also influence them to buy pictures of me wearing the panties. Then I'll message them the photos."

She includes handwritten notes to clients with the clothing items. One construction worker with a secret transvestite habit pays her extra money for her to let him send photos of himself wearing the dresses and shoes she has sent. Lady La keeps his interest by replying to the photos with insulting messages: "I'll tell him, 'That looks ugly on you. Your feet are too big for those shoes.' He loves it!"

Given her situation as a wife and young mother, doing physical sex work no longer appeals to Lady La. Not only does she not have time for it, but the stress involved in keeping such work private would take too much of a psychological toll, as would her lack of interest in sleeping with strangers, she says. "I wouldn't want to put myself through that mentally again."

However, at 18, had she not been engaged to be married and planning her future along those lines, she says she might have considered working in one of Nevada's legal brothels — several of which are within 20 miles of the greater Reno-Sparks-Carson City metropolitan area in northwest Nevada. Most young people growing up in the area are aware of these houses.

Lady La has no ethical problems with the houses. And she believes the spread of the Nevada model for brothels outside the Silver State is becoming more of a possibility. This is because of the growing economic disparity in the United States, and the financial challenges her peers in Generation Z face — the very same pressures that spurred her to take on a sugar daddy at 18.

What's more, her generation is more accepting of types of sexual behavior that older generations considered stigmatized, she says. As Zoomers reach adulthood and their political and social views carry more clout, it could influence the decriminalization and legalization of transactional sex, she says. And the change in legal status could include Nevada-style brothels.

"Eventually, it could be legal because of the older generations exiting — the ones who don't agree with it as much as our generation. We have literally been desensitized about sex. We're making sex for pay normalized.

"I'd say it's an eighty percent chance that brothels will be legalized across America in the next twenty years."

* * *

Bunni, former sugar baby, says sex-for-pay is so widespread, it should be legalized to protect practitioners and the public

AFTER SHE TURNED 18 and was struggling to afford living expenses as a college student in Reno, Bunni considered sex work — but not in one of the legal brothels in nearby rural counties. Growing up in northern Nevada, she'd heard rumors about a male owner exploiting the working women.

"I wasn't going to go there and be the little guinea pig they get to test out for free," says the blond, petite 23-year-old, whose photogenic features — high forehead, high cheekbones and large doe eyes — have helped her model professionally as one of her income streams.

Too, being a full-time college student, Bunni needed to be in control of her schedule, which precluded brothel work and its practice of having courtesans work two- to three-week shifts in residence. But after earning living expenses briefly as a sugar baby — paid by a sugar-daddy client — Bunni realized the advantages of security that a legal house provides. And she supports the widespread legalizing of Nevada-style brothels — as long as they are operated in a professional manner that respects the rights of the working women.

It's the humane — and logical — step to take, Bunni says.

"The biggest advantage is safety. If you look at abortion, you made it illegal but it's still happening. And it's happening unsafely — coathanger abortions in bathroom stalls. It's killing women. Legalizing the brothels would be giving women a safe spot to do what they're already doing. They still have the option to do it completely freelance — not with a brothel, not with a company, but under the table, illegally, in every state. But if we legalize it, we're giving women a safe space, and an opportunity where they will be tested regularly. That's not only keeping them safer, it's keeping their clients and the general population safer from STDs."

Bunni clearly remembers the anxiety she endured during her eight-month run as a sugar baby as an 18- and 19-year-old. "If I'm giving my sexual services to somebody illegally, and they assault me, drug me, rape me, or do something I didn't agree to, I have no protection, because I can't go to the cops," she says.

While she didn't experience physical abuse as a sugar baby, the feeling of vulnerability was constant for her — as it was for friends of hers who also put in time as sugar babies to support themselves in college. She's had similar trepidations as a model. "If you work as a freelancer instead of through an agency, you get hit up by a lot of creeps. Girls I know in my position, whom I've worked with, have been roofied."

These experiences underscore for Bunni the security benefits of a brothel structure for women willing to do courtesan work.

Her brief foray into transactional sex was spurred by seeing peers making ends meet as sugar babies: a growing phenomenon among women of her generation.

"I stumbled upon sex work when I was really struggling in college, and some of my friends were actually doing it through a website, SeekingArrangement, which now is called Seeking. I was a sophomore, and besides my classes I was working at an apartment complex and my duties were everything from being a leasing agent to heavy lifting of furniture. I have some health issues, and when they were getting worse, I had to find a way to work less while earning more.

"I was paying for my own tuition, my own apartment, my own food, my cat and his food, all my medical bills. I'd been working since I was thirteen, babysitting and dog walking back then, and I worked through high school as a tutor for children, and I bought a car at sixteen and got a credit card when I was eighteen to build up my credit rating. I've always hustled to support myself. My parents are working class and couldn't help me pay for college, so I was paying my way through school with the help of scholarships. I did not take out student loans. I don't like the idea of owing the government money, and I don't want to stress about debt. I always pay my bills up front. And when you do that, sometimes you gotta do a little extra to get by."

An idea for earning extra came when friends showed her the Seeking Arrangement website. The young women explained how they had found sugar daddies who paid them regular stipends for companionship.

'I stumbled upon sex work when I was really struggling in college,' Bunni says. 'Some of my friends were actually doing it through a website, SeekingArrangement, which now is called Seeking.'

"They were seeing, like, the highest rollers in the casinos, married men who lived in California that they would only have to see, maybe, once every three or six months, but they were getting weekly or monthly allowances," Bunni says. "I saw how they were putting in very short hours and getting their entire month's rent paid. They were doing something they would normally do for a man in a relationship, but they were being taken care of for it.

"Seeing them getting the benefits from it encouraged me to do it, although they did have some words of warning. 'Some of them are ugly.' 'Some of them are creepy.' 'Some of them are going to push your boundaries.' 'Some of them are not going to respect you.' I thought, 'Well, you're still doing it. Why can't I?' So I signed up and took a wild shot at it. I started reaching out to some sugar daddies and seeing who would reach out to me."

While some of her friends juggled multiple sugar daddies — lying to each that he was their only one — Bunni decided she'd be content with one single client to cover her financial needs. She was hoping an ideal sugar daddy would reach out to her: an out-of-towner she would have to see only once every six months when he traveled to her town or flew her out to see him, but who would provide her a weekly or monthly allowance regardless of whether they met up. These dream sugar daddies proved elusive, however. Most of the men who hit up Bunni online were lonely single men.

She met up with one local man. "He made me highly uncomfortable. He was fat as fuck. He said on his profile he was thirty-five. I'm guessing he was forty, maybe forty-five."

Bunni thought he'd be easier to handle than older sugar daddies, but during the eight months she saw him, he was manipulative. He'd take her to a Reno hotel-casino where he was comped suites as a big gambler but proved tight with his wallet when it came to paying for sex. He kept arguing about her price to lower it, Bunni says. "I didn't realize it's *my* price. I had set it higher on my profile than what I got, but I still had set it too low, and he knew that. I'm sure he had other sugar babies that he'd pay five hundred dollars a date — this was a few years ago, before sugar dating really became monetized. It's disgusting to me now, but he ended up bumping my price down to a hundred and twenty-five dollars, because I was eighteen and didn't know better. He was exploiting me and the fact I was very new.

"He'd always pay afterward, too, instead of in advance. That's the scary thing — there's no real insurance for sugar babies against getting ripped off. And there are a lot of scam artists, people who DM you online to get your account information. Many sugar babies do get paid upfront, but because so many sugar daddies have been getting scammed, many will not pay anything upfront.

"He also would not respect my decision to use condoms. And he was verbally abusive. He asked me, 'Have you had a kid before?' while glaring at my body. This fat white sausage was asking if I've had a kid before! And that's the last time I saw him."

I'm reviewing the weekly medical records for courtesans. *Photo by Jason Kelley*

It proved to be her last sugar-daddy date, too, although she kept her profile on the app. A few years later, the same man messaged her, perhaps having forgotten who she was. He offered her six thousand dollars a month to see him about once a month.

Bunni replied to his message: "You don't remember me, do you? You should have known my worth back then. You need to treat women better. You're disgusting."

The only other sex work she's done is sell nude photographs of herself. This did not come about by plan. Bunni simply accepted offers she was receiving from people who'd DM her on social media, offering her "an insane amount of money" for the photos. Selling the photos did trouble her, though, wondering where the images might be shared. "I never got too far with that, because you just can't trust what they'll do with the images."

These days, Bunni — who has become polyamorous — enjoys a stream of unsolicited cash or gifts from a variety of friends and lovers who simply enjoy her company. It's provided her a revelation about the companionship qualities of a woman:

"I can have a girlfriend who buys me a sweater. I can have a boyfriend who sends me five bucks for coffee, and the other who sends me ten bucks for tequila. I can have a best friend who buys me a plushy. If I'm valuable enough to these people that they want to buy me a forty-five dollar plushy that looks like a plant, I'm going to take it. I've realized that as women, there's a reason why we're not seen as the providers. Our worth is not in providing; it is so much more!

"We create a place that is this other person's *home*. Because home is not always a physical place. For a lot of people, their residence is a very traumatizing place. But when home is a *person*, it's comfort, it's familiarity, it's pleasure. We women can bring all that to the table, and it's valuable."

Bunni continues hustling for a living. She takes gigs as a model and a go-go dancer. She travels for a cannabis company, doing promo for their products. "It's easier to sell cannabis than to sell myself," she quips.

While she doesn't intend to sell sex — as she had as a sugar baby — she strongly believes transactional sex should be legalized and regulated. And she supports the Nevada model.

It's all about security and the freedom of choice, she says.

"If you're in a brothel, and someone's there onsite, running the books, managing the girls, checking in with them, it's safer. Is a customer really going to risk committing a crime, knowing he's given his ID when he pays for the party? This gives women that safe space in which to make consistent money. And giving them a separate space to do specifically sex work is extremely important. You don't want to be doing that in your own bedroom. You do not want people to know where you live. You don't want them to be able to target you, stalk you, because then you are subjecting yourself to possible sexual assault. If you're not in a brothel where you have the madam regulating everything, the chances of a woman getting beaten, drugged, raped, murdered even, seem so high."

Women who choose to do sex work should have the right to do so legally, Bunni says.

"Some people don't want to pay that price to have those safety measures. They want to keep working under the table, and not give control of their income over to the house and have it taxed. But the option should be there for women who want security, and who want to abide by the law. All women should have that choice if they want to work in a brothel, safely and legally. Because men are going to choose to come see us for these services, anyway.

"So many people are doing it. The sugar-daddy sites are not going away."

* * *

Sara: Escapee from an oppressive land savors freedom to explore her sexuality as a sex worker

SARA'S BACKGROUND DIFFERS STRONGLY from those of the eight other sex workers interviewed for this chapter. She attained political asylum in the United States to escape an oppressive marriage and sexist government. For this 33-year-old immigrant from Saudi Arabia, the idea of women choosing to earn money as sex workers in a legal brothel — where their health, safety and privacy are protected — is very appealing. It's all about a woman's freedom to have control over her own body and destiny, she says, and she fully supports my vision for the Nevada model for brothels being adopted across the United States.

"If a woman wants to work as a sex worker, it's like any other job. It's entertainment," Sara says. And she fully supports the Nevada model for brothels being adopted across the United States: "I'm with Bella on that."

Sara hasn't worked in a brothel, although she did contact me, inquiring about the logistics of coming to work at the Hacienda. To date, her sex work has been limited to stripping in a club in the large city in which she resides with her two children in the Western United States, and going out with one of the wealthy clients who engaged her services in the VIP room at that club, although their out dates have included only oral sex.

What attracts Sara to sex work is more than the income she can earn as a single mother who fled her native country and an abusive husband a few short years ago for asylum with her children in the United States. She also craves the experiences to be had as a means of self-discovery, after having spent her adulthood in an oppressive marriage in which her husband's needs, alone, were met in bed.

"I'm like a butterfly," Sara explains. "I want to explore my sexuality and find out what I want."

Sara came to America in a tide that is sweeping hundreds of Saudi women like her each year to Western nations such as the United States and Canada, Germany and Sweden, the United Kingdom and Australia. They escape a nation where women are notoriously controlled, despite reforms being made by its head of state, Crown Prince Mohammad bin Salman. He's permitted women to drive cars and attend sports events, and he touts efforts to make it easier for women to enter the workplace. Yet he's also jailed women's-rights activities who have pressed for ending the kingdom's guardianship system. This system renders women dependent on male relatives (typically a father or husband, but sometimes a brother or son) as if they were legal minors. A woman must obtain her guardian's permission to marry, travel, work, access healthcare, or even rent an apartment or file a legal claim.

When Sara was a teenager, her parents arranged her marriage to an older businessman. She says he physically and mentally abused her — including tugging her by her then long hair — harshly keeping her in the role of subservient housewife and caretaker of their children. But as with many women in repressive patriarchal societies, access to social media revealed to Sara the scope of her gender's oppression compared to women's freedoms in other nations.

With help from an international aid agency, Sara escaped from her husband several years ago and traveled with her children to Turkey, where she sheltered for eight months in a safe house. She eventually secured travel to the United States, where her "green card" visa allows her to reside and work permanently.

"I moved here with no good education," Sara explains. "I had my high school diploma but brought no documents or anything. I never had a career. I was just a housewife in Saudi Arabia. I came here having to be independent and strong and working without support or family. I had to find a job to provide things for my kids."

What attracts Sara to sex work is more than the income she can earn as a single mother who fled her native country for asylum in the United States. She craves the experiences to be had as a means of self-discovery.

Sara found a full-time job as a bank teller and supplemented it with part-time work as an interpreter, as she speaks four languages. The combined income wasn't enough. "I had to find another night job," she says. "I had to do what I'm doing now. I'm a dancer, a stripper. Sex work is just flexible time."

It was a wild and dramatic change from her former life as a cloaked housewife in Saudi Arabia. And Sara relishes the experience as an adventure as well as a provider of a decent income stream that fits her schedule as a single mother.

She sets her own hours. She makes good money. She hears the same words — "You look exotic" — from patrons who gravitate to her for lap dances in the main club area or private dances in the VIP room. They regard Sara's short, curvy body and olive skin, curly black hair (cut now to her neck) and her big brown eyes, and think she's Hispanic or Brazilian. In fact, she's a striking blend of Arab and East Indian heritage.

Such is her appeal that Sara frequently is asked by men or couples to perform sex acts with them in the VIP room. She declines. "I don't feel comfortable because it's not safe and not legal," she says.

Then there are customers who ask her to be their "sugar baby." They typically are looking for travel companions — which she wouldn't want to do, since she must look after her children — or arrange to meet her at her home, to which she won't agree, needing to preserve her family's privacy. But there is one silver-haired, distinguished-looking man whom she did agree to meet outside the club for companionship. The man, she learned, happens to be a high-ranking elected official in his state, and is married with children. His on-the-record politics cast him as a staunch conservative. Yet, his intimacy needs unfulfilled, he was desperate for sensual touch. Sara performed oral sex on their outdate, but she refused to go further. She says she feels no chemistry with the man.

That's not to say Sara would never consider taking on a sugar daddy — which other strippers at her club have, receiving expensive gifts, even cars. But there would have to be a real emotional connection and physical attraction, she says. One regular customer at her club has fit that bill, Sara says, but the two of them didn't discuss a sugar-daddy arrangement. However, the man did suggest a different career avenue for Sara. He recommended she check out my legal brothel. He had patronized Bella's Hacienda, and recommended it highly.

This tip led Sara to visit www.bellas.us, and then to contact me by phone. We had a nice long chat. Sara was intrigued and may take the plunge at some point.

"Bella's is a possibility," she says. "At strip clubs, some guys come into those places with diseases. At Bella's, they do testing, and make sure everyone does it the right way, with protection. And it's legal."

Then there's the emotional satisfaction she gleans from sex work, bringing joy to clients. At the strip club, she's felt gratified giving attention to lonely men, including some just released from jail, who are lonely, just needing someone to talk to, give them attention. "I'm a giver. Cancers are givers," she says, referencing her astrological sign.

Bella's, she understood from our chat, would bring her many different types of clients to nurture. And the variety would also allow her to explore different types of sex. Some of her favorite customers at the strip club are married couples in which the wives want to experience a woman's sensual touch. "The woman wants to dance with me, be touched by me, see if she likes it," Sara says. It helps her explore her own desires at the same time.

That, she says, has been long overdue: "I love exploring myself, finding what my body is, what intimacy is, what sex is. I was in an arranged marriage and had no control over my body or what I wanted to do. I'm enjoying my freedom now. It's my body. I don't care if anybody judges me."

> When Sara lived in the wealthy city of Abu Dubai, in the United Arab Emirates, she witnessed attractive foreign women obviously there as sex workers, even though the profession is outlawed by that nation's strict laws.

Sara views governmental restrictions on sex work as hypocritical and repressive. When she'd lived for a time in the wealthy city of Abu Dubai, in the United Arab Emirates, where her husband was conducting business, Sara witnessed attractive foreign women obviously in that country to ply their trade as sex workers, even though the profession is outlawed by that nation's strict Islamic laws.

"The government there is not brave enough to make it legal, but they know about what's going on," Sara says. "It should be legal, including here.

"If something happens between two adults and they're good with it, I don't know why the government should care."

* * *

NOW FOR THE OPINIONS of the five sex workers who have worked at Bella's, though they worked illegally in the trade before pulling stints at my house.

Kat, former streetwalker and escort, says brothels will be legal across the country in coming years

KAT IS UNEQUIVOCAL IN her support for legalizing Nevada-style brothels nationwide. "Hell ya!" she says. "It's the next step for the world order. It seems logical, doesn't it? It's almost Twenty Twenty-three. We evolve as humans."

For this 21-year-old who worked the streets of the San Francisco Bay area and online sites as an independent escort after turning 18, her experience at Bella's has convinced her of the advantages of the Nevada model for legal brothels.

"One of the plusses here at Bella's is knowing that in the environment I'm in, the people are healthy, and I'm being a good responsible sex worker going to the doctor once a week. I require everything to be safe and clean and protective."

For Kat, safety extends beyond customers using condoms and sex workers being tested. It includes safety from getting robbed — or worse. A couple of dates that went awry compelled her to take a family member's recommendation and apply at Bella's in the latter half of 2022. She's glad she made the change. Working as a brothel courtesan has proved her best income stream yet in sex work, and kept her focused on her goals of saving and investing.

Kat, of mixed ancestry, who touts her "exquisite curves and captivating eyes," got into sex work not long after graduating high school. She did work a minimum-wage job, sorting boxes for a shipping company. It wasn't enough to cover her expenses, and she didn't like simply trading time for money in a dead-end job. Growing up in an urban environment, as well as tuned into social media like the rest of her generation, Kat was well aware of sex work, and pondered whether it was better than the average 9-to-5 job.

"One of my acquaintances knew a little more than I knew about escorting, and she had other friends who knew more about the business. I wasn't blindly going into it. I had some structure. We started online and outside. For online, you create an advertisement for a site. For outside — the physical world — you can just mingle. You can work the 'catwalk,' the 'blade.' They have a few in the Bay area, and it was quite convenient."

("Catwalk" and "blade" are slang terms for a busy street known for strolling sex workers.)

Kat stepped into escort work using Eros.com. Cash immediately flowed. She'd either go on an outcall to meet a client or book a hotel room for the client to come to her. She booked rooms so often at one hotel in an upscale chain, she earned the status as a Diamond member, which afforded upgrades.

Kat was careful in screening clients. She used a variety of apps that provided information on them and, early on, had them send photos of their driver's license (with address blotted out). Her favorite clients were "hobbyists." "They are real businessmen who actually enjoy meeting women as a hobby. They have accounts and are verified, and it was much easier to book with them."

Kat had a backup for the periodic ebbs in online dates: streetwalking. "I liked to provide a nice place where my clients go, and if I didn't have the room fee, I could always go outside and make the money for a room. And if I had the room, but I wasn't getting much traffic on my phone, I could always go outside, dressed casually in a dress and normal heels, and someone would find me.

"You can catch someone's attention anywhere. You can literally be at the airport, and someone will find you. Opportunities are *everywhere*. Some people might see me outside and say, 'It's my first time, I've just seen you and you sparked my interest.' They're not looking for it, but if you just happen to be there and catch their eye, it's a different atmosphere."

There are, of course, perils to hustling outside — including pimps or their scouts who cruise the streets. Kat kept a keen eye on her surroundings. "There are a lot of people who work for people, who are recruiting new girls or take girls, a whole bunch of things. You don't even look their way, otherwise you're giving them the greenlight. If you don't know what you're doing, I would advise you to don't do it. But the people who are built for it, will last."

Kat lasted. She maintained a positive attitude. "I have faith in a higher power, much higher than me, so when I'm outside, I have no fears. I remember that as long as you are prayed up, you will be good to go. Anything that's not meant for me will pass me by. Anything that's meant to happen, will happen. Having that formulated in your mind is so grounding."

The sex work covered her apartment and other living expenses. Then two bad encounters led her to reconsider her line of work.

"The first one was outside, on the blade. I got picked up by a man. Usually, I performed the act in the vehicle. Or if I had a room, we'd come to my room. But he had his own place, in an apartment complex, and he apparently was the owner. We went into his apartment. And I just felt the energy, the vibes, and I was not feeling it at all. My intuitive thought was to leave. So I ran. I ran out his door, but he also had a building gate. I twisted it and twisted it, and unlocked it, and made it out that gate just before him. He was running behind me. He gets in his car, he's following me. I panicked. I went down the longest street on that block and I go into someone's yard, and they had a white picket fence, and I ducked down and covered my mouth. He was slowly passing by. It was like a horror movie. Luckily, I was out that night with two other female friends, and I texted one of them, and told her my location, and she came and picked me up."

The second date ended even more intensely.

Kat brought a young thug visiting from Chicago to her room — a demographic type she didn't normally cater to. "Chicago's pretty rowdy but I took a chance with this one," she says. Unfortunately, that wasn't her only lapse in judgment. "Rule number one, never leave your purse out. Rule number two, never show them where you put the money. That's two mistakes I made that night."

The young man's budget was limited, so Kat agreed to oral sex only. "We partied, and I did not include vaginal sex in the service because the pricing didn't meet the requirements," Kat says. "He wanted to rebook. He left for his car 'to get some extra.' Then he came back up. And he paid me the extra money. And I gave him five minutes, since I price range my time. But after I ended the party, shit got bad. He wanted his money back — and I don't give people their money back. I said, 'No, I don't give refunds.' He was a larger guy. He got really aggressive, so I gave him the money back he'd given me the second time. In those situations, I never want to get aggressive. I don't know if he has something on him or not.

"But I was upset. And I told him as he walked out the door, 'You should never make a girl uncomfortable like that again.' He put his foot in the door and pushed it open and went into my purse and took the money that was visible in the purse, then he ran out."

Soon after, Kat had a nightmare — and took it as an omen. "I had a dream that I was seeing a client and he had a firearm. I knew, 'No bueno, no good.' I took that dream into consideration and didn't even book another party."

Kat considered Nevada brothels. "I called Bella's, and everything was meant to be."

She started work at the Hacienda in August 2022. She planned on doing shifts over the next two years.

"Being here, I have a little more sense of security. And everything's legal. Yes, I pay taxes and split my profits, but being here in a brothel and knowing I don't have to communicate with clients directly to meet up with them or have them meet me, is simpler. I don't mind everything that comes with partnering with the house, because I know that all that I need will come to me in the correct time."

She enjoys being a courtesan.

"I like what I do. It's like an art form for me. I incorporate my spiritual practices into my work. I use terms like 'healing' and 'balancing.' I'm a spiritual being having a human experience, and the more people I share my energy with, I'm doing a favor for the world, and for myself. I take negative energy from other people and transform it into good energy.

"And when I do decide to do something else for the rest of my life, I will have the financial freedom."

What chance is there for Nevada-style brothels to be legalized elsewhere in the United States?

"I'd guess the odds are seven in ten," Kat says. "But if Bella is behind this endeavor, and she has the right intention and the energy is with her, there's no doubt in my mind that she will succeed. I'd say within the next five years, brothels will be legalized all around the United States. Outside the country, they're already doing it. They just gotta hop on the bandwagon here and get with the program.

"It always starts with an idea. And that will open up so many opportunities for ladies to work legally."

* * *

Claire says 'sexual healthcare' is a noble calling and sex work should be decriminalized, brothels legalized

CLAIRE CALLS SEX WORK "sexual healthcare."

"Sex work provides more than sex," she says. "It provides therapy, company, touch, words of affirmation that people need to hear. It's just really good for people's mental health. I notice some of my clients, who are nervous or depressed, afterward they are relaxed, calm, happy."

Sex work is a noble calling for a compassionate soul like herself. And it is helping her reach her financial goals. That's why she supports not only the legalization of regulated brothels across the country, but decriminalization for independent sex workers. She's worked both ways.

"I am usually more for decriminalization more than legalization, but I could also see how legalization could be beneficial to the women, because that involves testing and health checks and security," says Claire, a tall and slender 27-year-old with a cascade of kinky curls and a softspoken, mindful demeanor. She began working in October 2022 at Bella's Hacienda, specializing in the "GFE"— the tender, nurturing "Girlfriend Experience"— while also catering to clients with fetishes. Before that, she worked independently where she lived in the Tampa, Florida, area.

While her reasons for engaging in sex work are mostly financial, they include the gratification she gleans from providing therapeutic services to clients, and the opportunity to interact with a great variety of people. "It's interesting to get to know different types of people," she says, "even if they're people I don't want to be with."

Claire hardly grew up in a promiscuous environment. She had a chaste childhood, moving from her native Jamaica to Florida with her family at 14. She was not sexually active in high school. Still, the idea of transactional sex had piqued her teenage curiosity. Though her career thoughts at the time were to become a midwife, when given an English class assignment to research and write a paper about an occupation she was considering, she wrote about sex work, finding it more interesting.

Her first foray into monetizing her sexuality was after turning 16, "sexting guys for Amazon gift cards," Claire says. A regular customer was a "Splenda daddy" (a term for an older man interested in younger woman, but who isn't as wealthy as a sugar daddy) whose fetish was being teased with threats of blackmail.

"When I was 18, I decided to go into camming to move out of my mother's house with money," Claire says. She made an account on

MyFreeCams.com and produced strip-tease and other sexy streams. But that didn't generate enough to support herself. She also was pressured by her boyfriend — ironically, a man she met through the website —to quit camming. "He was very disapproving of that kind of work. He was very possessive of me."

Claire took a job at a clothing store in a mall, but still posted videos online by editing content she'd previously made. After breaking up with her boyfriend at 22, she began a relationship with a man older than her father, "to gain some freedom from the ex," she says. And she ventured into escorting.

"I talked with a girl I knew in the industry, and she gave me advice and I went into it independently," Claire says. She proved a quick study. She used escortdirectory.com and tryst.link to find dates and was able to make her rent money quickly. She boosted her knowledge about the occupation by chatting on an app with other escorts in central Florida. She learned to be scrupulous about security, running background checks on potential clients using VerifyHim.com, scanning for red flags, such is if the man was using a burner phone or text-plus service.

"I would ask for a picture of their ID. If they weren't comfortable in providing that, I would ask for their name and place of work," Claire says. "I would do video chats. If they were pushy about my boundaries — the services I wouldn't provide, and my requirement that they wear protection — that weeded out the bad guys."

For those who passed her screening, Claire would arrange a visit at a hotel or their home. Her boyfriend was her security backup: Claire shared the date's information and party location with him. "I had a system of checking in with code words — 'all good' if things were bad, and 'all gravy' if things were good. Nothing went wrong. I was pretty safe and cautious. I didn't have any bad experiences, really."

Although she turned down offers for visits under an hour, thus eschewing doing a higher volume of dates and the potential for more income, the work paid her well, Claire says.

"I got maybe two to three clients a week, which I was comfortable with. I charged three hundred and sixty dollars for an hour with regular clients. I was very, very happy with what I was making. I had a lot of money saved up. I had my own apartment.

"I did escort work for two years, then COVID hit. I decided to put it down, the escorting, because my health is more important. I moved in with my partner."

When Claire was 18, she decided to go into camming to earn money to move out of her mother's house. She made an account on MyFreeCams.com and produced strip-tease and other sexy streams.

The living situation ended acrimoniously. Claire moved back in with her mother. She struggled for money all over again. She ventured into web-camming and an OnlyFans site but found it difficult to generate income in those saturated fields. *Return to escorting?* Claire decided against it. She'd found the work stressful, always concerned about her personal safety and privacy, and the risk of potential stalkers. One person — not a client — had tried breaking into her home. Claire wanted to avoid exposing herself to such danger.

Intent on moving out of her mother's home, she began considering working in a Nevada brothel. She watched well-known Nevada courtesan Alice Little's YouTube channel. A TikTok video by another Nevada courtesan sparked her interest even more. Claire scrolled through brothel websites and applied to Bella's Hacienda. She started work at the house in October 2022 and stayed into December, with plans to resume in January.

She appreciates having the burdens lifted of having to market herself as an escort, to travel to see customers, to worry about security issues. Her earnings as a legal courtesan are comparable to the level she'd earned pre-pandemic as an escort, although the workload involves more clients. The diversity of ages and body types doesn't trouble her. The only clients she shies away from are those with strong body odor. The house environment generally suits her, too — with the exception of occasional disruptions of her sleep schedule by a house visitor at an odd hour, requiring a lineup.

"When the buzzer rings, the buzzer rings," Claire says.

She keeps her financial goals firmly in mind: "I would like to buy some land and build a house."

The market for customers is strong. The work is satisfying to her. The parties "feel more worthwhile and also fun" at the brothel, she says.

Legalizing brothels nationwide is an idea that appeals to her.

"There are lot of lonely men out there who have a negative view of women, because they haven't actually had any experience with women and accessible sexual healthcare. Accessible brothels would be great for that," she says.

It could prove a safety valve for society, as well. "When people are miserable, they are capable of some pretty terrible things."

But Claire doesn't expect Nevada-style brothels to be legalized elsewhere in the United States in the foreseeable future — unlike how the legalization of medical and recreational marijuana dispensaries has spread to 21 states and the District of Columbia since 2012.

"I think it would take a lot of years," Claire says. "I don't think it would be spontaneous, like weed is. Religious groups would oppose it. And I think a lot of people are sex-phobic."

* * *

Summer says all sex work should be legal but the Nevada brothel model appeals to her because of its security

SUMMER BELIEVES SEX WORK by independent contractors should be legal and regulated — period.

"At the end of the day, girls are going to be doing it anyways. If you can have it legal where they can do it in a safer way, where they are tested, I'm for the idea."

She applauds the Nevada model for brothels and wants to see it spread nationwide: "I think it's really genius." However, the 50 percent cut from a courtesan's earnings taken by the house in Nevada won't appeal to every prospective sex worker, she says. "It just depends on the girl. If they want to be an escort, they can do that, that's good. I like both ways. It's really up to the girl."

In Summer's particular case, the Nevada model suits her well. The security of a brothel — and the very fact it's legal — are major considerations.

"Since I've been in legal trouble before, in the juvenile system, doing drugs when I was younger, I never want to be in trouble with the law ever again. It's scary," says the 22-year-old green-eyed brunette with curly shoulder-length locks and a curvy body, who did her first stint at Bella's Hacienda in September 2022 and continued with more stints in the following months. She bills herself as "a warm ray of sunshine" and specializes in the "GFE" (Girlfriend Experience) of tender nurturing, while also enjoying servicing couples, as well as female clients either one on one or in "multi-lady parties."

Meanwhile, the safety of the environment suits her, given a bad encounter she'd had with a customer she'd met while stripping at a Seattle club. The income she's earning at Bella's is the clincher.

"The money has been really, really good," Summer says. "This has something to do with my age, being the youngest one here, and being pretty. Also, a lot of people tell me that once they meet me, they don't feel anything fake from me. They can tell I'm being a real human being."

That some customers are grossly overweight or otherwise physically unappealing does not bother Summer. Her work at a strip club in her native Seattle got her accustomed to the range of patrons. Courtesan work is not difficult, and the parties are interesting to her. "It's kind of fun to meet new people and just hear their story and what they're looking for and doing that for them. I don't do any of that crazy stuff. My parties are usually pretty simple. Oral sex and sex. I haven't had any customers yet that have wanted something really crazy."

She was less fortunate in Seattle, after an error in judgment led her to date a customer from the strip club who'd tipped her large.

Summer hadn't been working in the club for long. She was 21 and had craved a job change and better income from toiling in a pizzeria. "I was a cook for a really long time and was getting really stressed out from that job because it was really understaffed, so I started working at a strip club."

Summer found she preferred the grind of stripping to that of tossing dough — although she didn't jump full bore into the new line of work. "I was going through a lot in my life and was really unmotivated to do anything. I would show up there once in a while and make the money I needed to make my rent, and that was about it."

She quit at the strip club after a bad experience with one man she met there and started dating. "He ended up being a really bad person. He was violent and he essentially assaulted me," she says. She filed charges and the case was set for a trial date 10 months after the alleged incident. (This interview was conducted prior to that date.)

Summer vowed never to do an outdate with a virtual stranger again. However, trading sex for money was a positive experience for her when she slept with two different men she knew in her personal life and trusted: "I knew they weren't going to do anything crazy."

She decided sex work could be viable for her, were the environment secure. A fellow stripper at the Seattle club, who'd seen a TikTok video about Nevada's sex-worker laws, had planted the idea in Summer's head to research the brothels online. She determined that they *were* safe to work in.

Summer started her first shift at Bella's Hacienda in September 2022, intent on generating the strong income stream a brothel courtesan can earn. Her grand goal is to save enough money to create a nonprofit organization to assist people who — as she herself had — struggle with drug addiction and keeping a roof over their heads, and are committed to becoming sober and self-supporting.

"I did a lot of drugs when I was younger, and I moved into an Oxford House when I was eighteen," Summer says. "The rent is only five hundred dollars a month. It's really helpful."

Oxford Houses are a nonprofit network of about 3,000 self-supported, drug-and-alcohol-free halfway houses for people recovering from substance abuse. Summer's dream is buying a property in Seattle to create a similar venue. "I want to open up housing for homeless and recovering drug addicts and be able to provide them housing and jobs in the building. I want it to either be free or as cheap as possible for them to live there. I don't know how it's going to work yet."

The biggest drawback to working at the brothel, she says, is the sense of isolation between shifts in the tiny town of Wells. "I'm used to the city, being able to go do what I want to do, get in my car and go to the store, go get my nails done, hear live music and go clubbing."

Her earnings at the Hacienda please her greatly. And the notion of Nevada-style brothels spreading outside the state intrigues her. Her hometown would be a good place for them, she says. "Seattle is liberal, and I just feel like there's a lot of girls from Seattle in this industry. I've met several girls here who are from Seattle. And it's just a really big place."

The financial challenges faced by her generation — given inflation and the rising cost of living, a tight housing market and the ever-expanding gap between the haves and have-nots — could make the appeal of working in legal sex establishments quite popular, Summer says.

"My generation has to hustle more than other generations did. Most people in this generation won't even be able to buy a house, because of how much the cost went up from when our parents bought a house."

What of moral concerns about transactional sex? It comes down to personal choice — and that choice should be legal, she says.

"Everybody lives their own life, and everybody should be able to do what they want to do. If you don't like it, you just shouldn't come here. I personally like having sex with people. And it's not just about sex. It's about talking and building relationships with people who maybe need that type of affection in their life. If I enjoy doing it, then I can do what I enjoy, and you can do what you enjoy. If you don't like it, don't think about it. You do *you* and I do *me*."

Legalizing sex work — regulating it so it's safe — including by independent operators outside of brothels, deserves to come about, Summer says.

"It would be important for the girls' safety, so the girls can be tested every single week, and we can get rid of the dangers that lead to the girls who go missing, and all the girls who have pimps and get beat up and can't get out of that lifestyle because their pimp is controlling them.

"If it were legalized, the girls can be safe and get their money for themselves, and know their money is going right into *their* bank account."

* * *

Millie: Liberty lover says legalization would invite governmental control — but make sex work safer

MILLIE SEES THE IDEA of decriminalizing transactional sex as a double-edged sword — and ditto for legalizing Nevada-style brothels across the country. Each concept would make sex work safer for providers and clients, yet enable governments to control how sex workers earn their income, and take a slice of that income.

"Decriminalizing it throughout all states and territories would create greater revenue, but would also mean greater oversight, greater restrictions, greater regulation, and greater overhead for the practitioners, says Millie, who, after she hit 18, began working under the radar as an independent escort in California, finding clients through online sites. After a dozen years, she opted to work at a legal Nevada brothel —

Bella's Hacienda — in 2022, having been worn down the by the grind of drumming up and maintaining business on her own and coping with the ever-present risk.

Weighing decriminalization or legalization against the status quo of criminalization, Millie tilts the scales toward the former. It's a matter of personal liberty and safety, she says. What's more, it would pencil financially for governments, which would realize more income from regulatory fees and taxes than they do from prosecuting violators of prostitution laws, she says.

"Absolutely it should be legalized in the sense that bodily and financial autonomy should not be infringed upon by anyone, especially the corporate government. For me, it paves the way to provide a safe platform for women in the industry to conduct their business in, and it's safe for clients, too. Having it criminalized creates dangerous environments for all parties involved. Is the risk that's involved really worth the bankroll that governments get from citing people and locking people up for solicitation?"

Ultimately, calculating the bottom line will determine whether decriminalization or legalization will spread, Millie avers. "The government is a corporation and operates as one. It's going to weigh which is generating a greater revenue stream — keeping it criminalized or legalizing it with its own three-letter agency, and with sex workers paying for permits and licenses and taxes. But safety should be of the utmost concern. It's a necessity. These are people's lives."

A constant in Millie's life has been a powerful sex drive coupled with strong curiosity — making sex work a natural fit for her. Her appearance helps her attract clients. The 30-year-old is an olive-skinned ethnic mix: Irish and German ancestry on her mother's side, Navajo and Mexican on her father's. Standing 5-foot-1, busty with a 38DD chest, Millie has a voracious appetite for sex, and sex work seemed like a natural path for her from an early age.

"It was something I was familiarized with because my mother did a lot of sex work to support my sister and me. We were heavily exposed to it. There was a developed sense of normalcy to the idea."

What also was normal, unfortunately, in her childhood was upheaval. Born in New Mexico, Millie and her older sister were raised there in their early years by their mother, after their father, a heavy drinker, left the family. Millie's mother did sex work to feed her daughters and afford a hotel room. At 7, Millie and her sister moved to the Los Angeles area and lived with their father and paternal grandmother. After their grandmother passed, the girls ended up in the custody of an older cousin. Millie finally found a stable living arrangement in the home of the mother of her best friend from school.

Her libido raged from an early age. "I was a hypersexual child and teenager. I'd known I liked women since I was four. I knew that very distinctly. I didn't know I was bisexual until I was eleven or twelve, when I knew there were gay people and straight people. I had never identified myself as that until I got my first girlfriend, and we kissed in the locker room. And everyone at school was insulting me, calling me a 'dyke,' 'lesbian whore,' every kind of degrading expletive."

Millie, though, burned to continue exploring her sexuality. And legal adulthood afforded her ample opportunity. "When I turned 18, I had the legal liberation from the people who were caretaking me. I had this sense of exploration. It was the most hedonistic, excessive approach I could take to exploring my sexuality. It's not a healthy way, but I discovered the easiest way to access it. I discovered webcams and chat sites and started with that. Then I discovered Craig's List, 'casual encounters' in the Personals section. From there, it took off."

Looking back, she understands she was reckless, sometimes putting herself in dangerous situations, which at its root was triggered by dealing with childhood trauma. Nevertheless, her escapades taught her a great deal about herself, and revealed a source of income to her. People she hooked up with were willing to compensate her.

"I was getting paid for something I wanted and was seeking to do. I was looking for sex, so it was easy to figure out how to get paid for it." Millie worked briefly in other occupations — as a body piercer, a manager of a store in a tattoo parlor, and as a healthcare worker with elderly patients in rehabilitation centers, long-term care and hospice. But she found that sex work, as a self-described "independent escort" paid much better — and was much more to her liking.

> A constant in Millie's life has been a powerful sex drive coupled with strong curiosity — making sex work a natural fit for her. Her mixed-ethnic appearance and busty 38DD chest helps her attract clients.

Craig's List shut down its Personals section — the giant back-page network — in 2018, and Millie migrated to dating sites such as Tinder, Seeking, and WhatsYourPrice, often getting banned because her profiles were too direct. She adapted. "I learned how to navigate a lot of sites. I stuck to the ones that I know would generate traffic for me."

But the unstable stream of income, the grind of building a buzz on a site, the wearying wariness of working in an illicit trade, wore on her. After a living situation ended with an older man, a lawyer, in San Francisco, Millie moved into her own studio apartment. Then she decided she was sick of living in the big city. She happened to see a TikTok video by a young woman who worked in a brothel in southern Nevada. Millie scrolled through brothel websites and ended up on the phone with me. She decided to give legal sex work a shot.

"I saved up, sold all of my stuff to get out here," she says. The relief of not having to drum up clients online, or live off a sugar daddy, she adds, is profound. The legal courtesan life suits her. "I'm finally at a point in my life where I have financial autonomy now, not depending on anyone else. And now that I have the environment to do so in a legal fashion, I can pursue it seriously as a career. There are some things I enjoy doing in the brothel, but not outside the brothel, where there is greater risk and much more management of yourself and the client."

Millie specializes in the "GFE" (girlfriend experience), pleasuring female clients (including "multi-lady parties") and kinky BDSM (bondage, discipline and sadomasochism). Working in the safety of a brothel allows her to conduct work she sees as benefitting clients more profoundly than sexual gratification. She delves into a client's psyche to figure out what the client really needs. If she can provide a positive experience, she gleans value apart from the monetary.

"As far as services I provide, it's an umbrella approach, things that are more kink and fetish oriented. Someone has some type of paraphernalia that they want to explore, or carries a lot of shame about, I will gladly cater to them, help them grow. I understand their needs. Growing up through my own explorations and discovering what aroused me before I understood it, I carried a lot of shame and embarrassment. I felt I was never going to be able to connect to another human being in a normal sexual way.

"If I'm able to create a moment for someone in which they feel that liberation of sexual freedom — even for just for a moment — in which they aren't berating themselves or seeking arousal in something not handled in a safe way, I think that's very meaningful and impactful. And not just through the arousal in the situation. It can be very healing. There's a great deal of therapy and healing that can be done, not just through sex or sex work, but being able to have a space in which you can share yourself freely, be emotionally, sexually free. To feel safe and liberated.

"It's huge for individual development, especially if you're someone who experienced a life of repression, to the point that your whole attitude toward sex and sexuality is negative. The weight that you bear from that attitude toward yourself completely disrupts your whole sense of self and how you operate in the world. There's a great deal of importance that I see to have safety in an environment in which you can be sexually liberated."

Millie also appreciates the simple business arrangement of being a courtesan — an independent contractor — in a legal brothel. It saves her from having to create an online brand and network anew, each time she's booted off a dating website, "getting people to find you in a very oversaturated market."

"The amount of time and energy you spend doing that for yourself, you might as well get a nine-to-five job for a wage," she says. But when you work in a brothel, you already have a brand, it's established, the clients know where to find you, you're not alone, you're not meeting a stranger off site, you have a sense of security, you have all their information if they pay with a card. There's a different approach, a different level of respect for people who understand what they're doing. There are so many benefits to it that makes it so much easier. Having a space to be based out of, it's like having a business office. The rent I pay to Bella is much more affordable for me than to do business outside of there, and to have separate travel expenses and overhead, and the risk. I live alone, travel alone, don't drive.

"For me and my lifestyle, working at a brothel is the best for me, best for my lifestyle, the safest, and it gives me the greatest amount of income, as well. I don't have to meet a random stranger at a random hotel and walk into a hotel room where there could be one guy or ten. It's an office where you can professionally conduct yourself with a client, and I prefer that. We can discuss everything we're going to do, and it leaves less room for someone to take control of the situation from me."

All that is worth more to Millie than losing out on portions of her income that she pays out to the house to cover overhead, to the local government in the form of license fees and to Uncle Sam for income tax, and worth more than the hassle of having to adhere to the strict laws to which she must abide, from regular health checks to abiding by house rules.

The benefits outweigh the detriments, she says. "If you're an escort with an established client base, you have your set price, your repeat customers. It's like having a small business that does tailoring, and you can survive off your twelve clients. But if you're an escort hustling everywhere, you are at great risk.

"My biggest thing is autonomy. Be it financially, my body, whatever. You own yourself; it cannot be commodified by anyone else. What you choose to do with your body, there should be no oversight over that. The government doesn't need to be involved with that. Decriminalization or legalizing gives the government as many tentacles as it can to get as much revenue as it can. That, for me is troublesome. That being said, I have made far more money being at the brothel than if I worked independently with that great of risk."

But the forecast for decriminalization, much less Nevada-style legalization, of sex work in the United States remains murky, Millie says.

"Within my peer group, what I see online and in interacting with people, there is a sense of a push to support sex work and sex workers. There is more or a less a growing attitude to support sex workers, which is nice. But I don't know what it looks like in other states, and what the attitude looks like on a legislation level. I'm surprised that California, being California, has not done it. The only reason I think it has not been done is because the state and federal governments have not found a way to transition it financially. At the end of the day, that's all it comes down to. The people who own those prisons, they care about their money, keeping them full. I see that as an obstruction to allowing sex work to be legal.

"But if it were legalized, it would divest people of this archaic taboo of transactional sex, that it's selling a person's body. Any job is transactional, including jobs that demand physical work. A construction worker who works eighty hours a week and retires with torn tendons and arthritis is just as much of a 'whore' as I am. Or someone in the NFL or NBA, and frankly, I wouldn't put my body in harm's way at the cost of concussions and neurological damage. There should be no connotation to the word 'whore.' There needs to be a different appreciation and understanding of sex work.

"Sex work is skilled work, like any service work. And it can be highly skilled service work, given how diverse it is."

* * *

V — a competitive earner who doesn't want brothels to spread elsewhere

FOR V, THAT NEVADA is the only state in the Union with legal brothels is to her benefit. It's a numbers game, she says. Legalize it elsewhere? That would increase competition and compromise her ability to earn more at Bella's.

"Do I have a problem with it being legal? No. Do I want it to be legal? No." says V, a 22-year-old dark-haired Chicana beauty with high cheekbones and full lips, who stands only 5-foot even but has a big presence. She's bisexual and has a rowdy side that fits right in at biker rallies, and a playful side that relishes role-playing and costumes.

She also has a businesslike mind fixed on the bottom line:

"There are only so many brothels here in Nevada," V explains. "I can charge a dude a thousand bucks for a particular party, and he can't say, 'I can get it anywhere.' I don't want to share my clients. I have customers who come from afar, like Colorado. I'm just being very honest. I'm not mature enough to think, 'Spread the wealth.'"

Not that V expects Nevada's model for legal brothels to be adopted outside of the Silver State any time soon. Politicians will continue shying away from legalizing brothels due to opposition from religious conservatives, as well as from a broad section of women, V says. "All these women who have husbands and sons and don't want to see legal prostitution, they're going to be against it."

And then there are sex workers themselves. "You can't expect all strippers are for brothels legalized, either. They're in competition, too."

V started stripping the day she turned 18 in her native Colorado. Her mother's career influenced her. "My mother was a stripper. I remember, when I was 13, my mom also did sex work illegally. She'd meet a guy in a hotel lobby, take him to her room, then go back down and wait for the next guy."

V wasn't initially raised by her mother. "I had a weird upbringing," she says. "I lived out on a farm with my grandparents because my parents were in prison when I was little. Then I went to stay with a foster-care woman, then moved in with my real mom at age eleven, in Denver. I had a rough childhood with her, and constantly was in group homes in Denver or on the street."

When V was 12, she was taken in by a family with a daughter her age, rescuing her from homelessness. She thinks of them as her adoptive parents, though they never legally adopted her.

V doesn't expect Nevada's model for legal brothels to be adopted outside of the Silver State any time soon. Politicians will continue shying away from legalizing brothels due to opposition from religious conservatives and a broad section of women, she says.

"I almost knew, ever since middle school or even younger, I was going to be a sex worker," V says. "It was something that caught my eye. For my eighteenth birthday, my gift to myself was two thongs, a dress and a pair of heels."

The first strip clubs she auditioned at were known as higher-end venues in Denver. They didn't have shifts available right away, so V sought out a less fancy club. Its manager told her to "turn around." "I did a three-sixty, and he said, 'You got the job, you work double shift.' I was there from two in the afternoon until two a.m., making my money, maybe five hundred dollars that first night. I was very excited."

At the time, V was dating a 26-year-old man who'd done six years in prison. He wanted to start a new life elsewhere. "We hitch-hiked and walked all the way from Colorado to Missouri," V recalls. "Long story short, I got the absolute shit beat out of me by him, and I ended up going back to my adopted mom and dad. I started dancing again and saving up my money."

Besides stripping, V worked for two fetish clubs and took go-go dancing gigs at motorcycle rallies around the country. She also worked for an escort party agency. While she saw co-workers do illegal sex-for-pay side hustles, V never did. Her only forays into transactional sex were two encounters with men she met on Tinder.

"I was very hungry for more money than I was making at the strip club, and didn't want to compete with those girls there, so I decided to explore it, like my mom had used to. I met with two of them. The first paid me three hundred dollars. The second one was supposedly a firefighter. He ended up bull-shitting me and left without putting the money down."

V nearly had her revenge on the deadbeat. Apparently, he was married. He accidentally pocket dialed photos to a random number in V's burner phone. The person with that number messaged V at one of her social-media accounts, asking what the photos were for. V had the contact send her the number that had sent the photos. She called that number. "A woman answered. I chickened out on saying anything."

The negative experience killed off V's appetite for sex-for-hire hookups via apps. But becoming a mother and wife has increased her ambition to earn a good income. When V was 20, a young man her age who worked with her adopted dad started dating her, and she got pregnant two weeks later. They married after their baby boy was born two months before V turned 21 in 2021. They rent an apartment in a complex where her husband is a maintenance man.

Having a home and family of her own has made V even more determined to drive toward financial goals. The pandemic had severely reduced her stripper income, and she decided to quit strip clubs after she asked the manager of her club if she could become a cocktail waitress. He asked her into his office and drunkenly tried coercing her into a private dance.

"I want to live a life that isn't just to survive," V says. "I want to flourish. I want it all. I started looking at all the Nevada brothels." The house rules spelled out in the contract at one large, well-known Nevada brothel made V nervous. "It's a lockdown house," she says, alluding to curfews and restrictions on leaving the house during a stint. Bella's freer policies appealed to her.

She pulled a two-week stint in July 2022 and returned each subsequent month.

"I'm doing amazing," she says. "Even though I still talk to my real mother — I love her though she's a nutcase — I'm able to send her money. I take care of my adopted family. I just gained custody of my 16-year-old half-brother, and he lives with my husband and me. I'm making more money than ever. I have goals and I have money to make there."

V's financial goals include paying cash up front for a nice house to accommodate her family and three dogs, paying off the house and buying a second as a rental unit. She intends to build generational wealth to bequeath to her son. She also wants to start a business making and selling "weird clothing/performance outfits," employing her sewing skills.

V plans on working at Bella's until she can reach these goals. "Until then, I'm going to keep coming back until there's no more money to be made, or my own business is making bank."

And as long as Nevada maintains its U.S. monopoly on legal transactional sex, she won't face stiff competition from beyond the Silver State's borders. V isn't worried about that.

"Based on being in the sex industry, if people are still so uptight even about strip clubs being by their houses and in their neighborhoods, and with police coming in and hassling dancers for even wearing pasties, it probably won't happen until I'm much, much, older, probably in my forties or fifties, or even older."

*　*　*

AND SO I HAVE shared the perspectives from nine different women in contemporary America who've earned money selling sex, about the potential benefits and possibility for legalizing transactional sex,

Nevada style, across the United States.

The biggest takeaways from these interviews are these points:

- Illegal transactional sex is widespread in 2020s America. It is not going away.
- Sex workers understand that the Nevada model of legal brothels offers safe, secure environments for transactional sex.
- Some sex workers aren't interested in giving up portions of their income by working in a legal brothel, where they would have to pay licensing and fees, and their earnings would be split with the house and be subject to income tax. Others say that's a reasonable tradeoff for the advantages of plying their trade in a secure environment that also relieves them of the costs of advertising and either travel or providing a location for conducting business.

It will be interesting to see how the decriminalization movement progresses in our nation during the remainder of the 2020s — not only in the states where bills are being considered, but in those that have yet to see local legislation introduced. And for myself, it will be fascinating to see which jurisdictions strongly consider legalizing transactional sex in some form — including adopting the Nevada model.

All I can say with assurance is — to quote Bob Dylan — the times they are a-changin'.

CONCLUSION

The Time for Sexual Evolution Is Now

Whenever I see a customer at Bella's Hacienda Ranch return to the bar after a party with a courtesan, glowing with a huge smile and a sense of lightness, I glow inside, too. The customer has not only experienced a precious episode of human joy — he or she has gained a lasting memory, a happy mental video, to draw on in the future.

In fact, the customer's experience has been more than physical. It has been *spiritual*. It has been a soul-to-soul connection on a basic human level: a transaction between two individuals, each of whom knew what he or she wanted, and what he or she was willing to give or get, with the understanding it was a win-win situation.

The gratification of sensual desires — the need for intimacy and human contact — will always be among the most basic of human needs. No number of laws has ever effectively quashed the world's oldest profession. Nor should they.

Allow me to quote from a highly educated courtesan who's worked at Bella's Hacienda Ranch. Her stage name is Janet. She is a multilingual European who immigrated to America in her teens and earned a graduate degree. Janet has worked off and on at the Hacienda since 2012.

Here's her take on the healing qualities of sensual services:

"Sexuality — the sexual drive and the need for physical intimacy — is an essential powerful force of life. Satisfying and unblocking sexuality has a creative, self-affirmative and energizing effect on people. In contrast, suppressed needs for sexuality and sensual touch can have severely negative or destructive effects on humans."

This is so true! And allow me to share this point:

Clients and sex workers are not doing anything that is not happening in bedrooms all over the world. One can make a moral judgement on anything, but unless what happens in the bedroom is illegal, sex workers and clients should be able to engage in intimate acts freely, safely and legally.

FORTUNATELY, HISTORY IS ON the side of the humane approach to legalizing the sensual-services industry.

The late Dennis Hof, who owned the Moonlite BunnyRanch in Mound House, Nevada, as well as six other brothels in northern and southern Nevada, offered this prognostication in his memoir published in 2015, *The Art of the Pimp: One Man's Search for Love, Sex, and Money*:

"I know prostitution will never be widely legalized. Any intelligent politician knows it's the right thing to do, but he's not going to stand up in front of Congress, or the PTA, or his church group and tell them what he really thinks. To speak his or her true feelings would be an act of political suicide."

With all due respect to the late Mr. Hof, "the right thing to do" *can* be done. The world *does* change. It *is* changing. In America, social taboos that were outlawed for ages eventually gain acceptance and become legal after shifts in public sentiment. Change often comes slowly, yet it comes. In my grandparents' lifetime, women in the United States won the right to vote. In my parents' lifetime, the sale of alcohol was legalized. In my lifetime, there have been desegregation, the widespread legalization and

Nearly four decades as a madam has given me plenty of perspective and vision about the legal sex industry – and humankind's need for intimacy. *Photo by Brandi Betancourt*

regulation of gambling, the legalization of same-sex marriage, and the legalization and regulation of medical and recreational marijuana in a growing number of states.

Legalizing prostitution may carry a much more explosive emotional charge than the other once-taboo issues. In fact, the subject of prostitution has strongly divided feminists. In their book, *Sex and Stigma: Stories of Everyday Life in Nevada's Legal Brothel*, published in 2019, co-authors Sarah Jane Blithe, Anna Widerhold and Breanna Mohr noted the "deep split" in the debate. As their book said: "Many radical-cultural feminists believe that women who are prostitutes are not simply selling sex, but that the act of prostitution makes them complicit in creating women as sex objects, which hurts all women." But their book also noted the other side of the argument: "Sex-positive feminists see empowerment and freedom for the women who choose prostitution as an occupation."

I stand squarely with the sex-positive feminists who — the authors wrote — "believe that prostitution can be empowering because prostitutes hold more sexual power when selling sex than in any other sexual situation between a man and a woman. Feminists embracing a sex-positive perspective claim that sex workers get to choose how much they charge and which clients they service, and that the power to make those decisions is not oppressive for the women."

And the authors made one additional point about the pro-prostitution feminists:

"Some sex-positive feminists realize that women who take ownership over and explore their sexuality through prostitution might actually push against the patriarchal norm."

In other words, by taking control of their sexual power to turn a profit, sex workers — courtesans — are involved in a progressive rebellion against male dominance in society.

This is the essence of female empowerment.

IF THE CASE I'VE made in this book has persuaded you to at least consider that the Nevada model of legal brothels can transform the world's oldest profession into a safe and well-regarded occupation — one that not only betters the lives of sensual-service providers but contributes vitally to the welfare of the human race — I invite you to support sexual evolution.

The time is right, and the time is now. Together — with capable courtesans providing sensual services to patrons who benefit greatly from them, and can safely and easily access them — the sexual evolution can transpire: making a better world for all of us.

My dream — a vision still unthinkable to most people — is to propel humanity forward by humanizing sensual services and the responsible gratification of sexual desires. Our species is evolving to colonize the stars. But down here on Planet Earth, we can learn to be much happier in our own bodies. We can learn to be human correctly.

Moving the brothel business out of the Dark Ages and into the 21st century is an evolutionary step for humankind.

Let the sexual evolution begin!

"While the difficult takes time, the impossible just takes a little longer."

— **Art Berg**

Saddled up for a ride on Beauty. *Photo by Lance Cummins*

ABOUT THE AUTHOR

Bella Shauna Cummins, an Illinois native, grew up in New York state in a large middle-class family, majored in agriculture at Panhandle State College in Goodwell, Oklahoma, and subsequently worked as a waitress, hotel-maintenance engineer, short-order cook, horse trainer, manicurist, department-store cleaner, restaurant proprietor-operator, and owner-operator ("madam") of a legal brothel: Bella's Hacienda Ranch, in Wells, Nevada.

A mother and grandmother, Bella resides with her husband, thoroughbred horse Beauty, goat Arrietti, three orphaned cats and two Airedale dogs on a ranch in northeast Nevada.

Bella is the longest-serving madam of a legal brothel in the United States. She advocates for legalizing and humanizing, nationwide and worldwide, what she calls "the sensual-services industry."

Sexual Healers: Hidden Secrets and True Values of the Legal Sex Trade is her first book.

www.ingramcontent.com/pod-product-compliance
Lightning Source LLC
Chambersburg PA
CBHW042318090526
44583CB00024BA/3027